A Glory Here

BY

PAUL BASSETT

AMBASSADOR

A Glory Here
© 1994 Paul Bassett

All rights reserved

ISBN 1 898787 06 9

Published by
AMBASSADOR PRODUCTIONS LTD.,
Providence House
16 Hillview Avenue,
Belfast, BT5 6JR
Northern Ireland
United Kindom

Acknowledgement

I wish to acknowledge my indebtedness to the late Gordon Sayer, the Librarian of the Evangelical Library and the staff for their assistance. I especially wish to thank Mrs. Rowe for the many hours of work she has put in typing the original manuscript.

Lastly I wish to say how grateful I am to the known and unknown people who have prayed that I might see heaven open.

Rev. P.T.A Bassett

*Dedicated to
all Heaven seekers*

Contents

1. Heaven Begins Here 9
2. Heaven Begins Now 13
3. Heaven - The Home of God 27
4. Heaven - News from Below 37
5. Heaven - Time of Departure 47
6. Preparing for Departure 57
7. The Ascent 67
8. What Heaven is Not 83
9. What Heaven will Be 99
10. Heaven - A New World 113

Preface

Never, perhaps, was there a time when man was more dissatisfied with earth. Never was there such a time as this, when man was restlessly reaching out beyond the confines of earth, exploring space, leaving the peak of conquered Everest far below. Once the moon was man's ultimate destination, but where now? Yet, amazingly, with all this space exploration, man has never written less about heaven, never thought less about it and never spoken less about it. Oh! yes, we recall the Russian astronaut Gaugarin saying he did not see God out there. And John Glenn is supposed to have retorted caustically that his God was too big to have been seen there.

The immediate thrust of this book is that heaven begins here. This earth is meant to be a place of preparation for heaven, and a time of preparation for eternity.

I believe heaven is much nearer to us than we think, and that it is actually possible to live in heaven whilst on earth. Yet this book was written with my feet firmly on the ground, and my heart, I hope, in heaven.

It is my conviction that the world and the Church need more heavenly-minded men, women and young people. History reveals that the most heavenly-minded Man did the most earthly good, and He was the Lord Jesus Christ.

Paul Bassett

"My extremity hath sharpened the edge of His love and kindness ... I would desire no more for my Heaven ... while I am sighing in this house of clay, but daily renewed feasts of love with Christ, and liberty now and then to feed my hunger with a kiss of that fairest face ... Nay, but I find that it is possible to find young glory and a young green paradise of joy, even here."

~ Samuel Rutherford
Aberdeen, 1637

1

Heaven Begins Here

In a Christian's understanding of heaven, it is normal for him to conceive of it as purely a future state. There appears to be little place in his thinking for heaven to begin here. In fact it begins where you are sitting or standing at this moment. Look up and being to see things in a new way. I suggest to you that the old way was merely to view sky and space, but you can begin this day to see God and heaven. For, "The heavens declare the glory of God and the firmament sheweth His handywork" [1]. In a sense, every time we see the beautiful blue sky, or even the grey one, it should convey to us the sheer wonder and beauty of our God. It should make us realise that He wants to move into our world and make heaven as much a reality to us as the earth beneath our feet. We were never meant to see God's world without seeing Him in it. It should, when we see the canopy of the spreading sky above us, make us see heaven too.

Of course we are only viewing the physical heavens, literally 'the heights', that which is above, but these must be our starting point. The opening and closing of each day is meant to be a glorious event in our lives in this mundane here and now. Every day should remind us as we close our doors behind us and step out into the world, that God is alive in heaven, for "day unto day uttereth speech" [2].

Behind the new day we should hear the voice of the speaking God desiring to be a contemporary person in our lives. And before we turn out the light on the dying day, let us equally realise as we view the starry sky above us that, "Night unto night sheweth knowledge" [2] that God is the God of the night as well as of the day. We were never meant to let a day go by on this planet earth without constant thought of God and heaven breaking in upon us. But of which of us can it honestly be said that this is true? It is possibly to live so blindly, as not to have God and heaven in our vision, and to forget totally or disbelieve it that "In the beginning God created the heavens and the earth" [3] in that order. Until man begins to see the heavens above, he does not really understand, nor see himself in true perspective.

We must learn to stand again with the young shepherd boy long ago, who exclaimed in awe and wonder, "When I consider thy heavens and the work of thy fingers, the moon and the stars which thou has ordained, what is man that thou art mindful of him and the son of man that thou visiteth him" [4]. At that moment we should see ourselves as we really are; in our creaturehood and sheer insignificance, beside the heavens above. It should be a thing of astonishment to us that God who made the heavens, can deign to think upon man, let alone visit this earth in the person of Jesus Christ. Surely man has such a great and proud view of himself because he has ceased to meditate upon the heavens above. When he does so, he will not only begin to see himself as a very unimportant dot in the universe, but he will be driven to recognise the incredible gulf that exists between the thoughts and ways of God and those of man. For God informs us, "My thoughts are not your thoughts, neither are your ways my ways saith the Lord. For as the heavens are higher than the earth, so are my ways higher than your ways and my thoughts than your thoughts" [5]. For too long man has had the audacity to measure almighty God by the crooked yardstick of his fallen and unenlightened mind. The only hope for man is to realise the gulf between the finite mind of mortal man and the infinite mind of the omnipotent God in heaven.

RAIN & SNOW FROM HEAVEN

Again man so often complains about the weather. Seldom is he found like the famous song, 'Singing in the rain'; rather is he to be found 'murmuring.' Oh! that when the next rain drop falls freshly on our faces, or splashes in the pool beside us, we would realise immediately who sent it and see it as "... the rain that cometh down from heaven" [6]. It is actually possible next time you are caught in the chaos on the roads due to a winter blizzard of snow, to discern in it the hand of God, for not only is every snow flake a unique creation of God, differing from the others in divine pattern, but it is "Snow from heaven" [7].

Even with all his twentieth century technology and with all the snow ploughs at his disposal, God in heaven "Sealeth up the hand of every man that all men may know his work" [8]. The wild beasts seem to have more sense than man and "Go into dens and remain in their places" [9]. Did you know, in fact, that the snow literally falls on the earth in obedience to the command of God, for "He saith to the snow, 'Be thou on the earth'" [10].

Returning to the rain for a moment, one discovers that whereas man bottles milk, God bottles rain. God sets us an incredible question - "Who can number the clouds in wisdom, or who can stay the bottles of heaven?" [11]. Once you view the heavens above in this way, you will never blame or even occasionally thank the 'Met' man for the weather, but realise as never before, that "He maketh His sun to rise on the evil and the good, and sendeth rain on the just and on the unjust" [12]. Even when we bring God 'into the picture', we generally blame Him for the bad weather and are like the lady in the post office (incidentally typical of millions) who exclaimed, "What have we done to deserve this?" The simple answer is that we do not deserve anything, do we?

You know, if we were to look up and follow the flight of the birds more often many of our troubles would fly away. How? do you ask? Well, Christ told man in His day to do just that. "Behold the fowls of the air, for they sow not, neither do they reap, nor gather into barns. Yet your **heavenly** Father **feedeth** them. Are ye not much better than they?" [13]. In the light of this provision, God rebuked men who needlessly carried the concerns of everyday life - what shall we eat, drink or wear? If heaven provides for our feathered friends, how much more for a man or woman who trusts in the living God?

God's care for the birds is also shown in their sense of timing. To illustrate this, all one has to do is to see the storks gathering on a September day in Alsace, France. Leaving their quaint nests on the house tops, they circle in the sky until their leader starts them off on their long migratory flight to the warmer climes of Africa. The Bible comes alive before our very eyes. "Yea the stork in the heavens knoweth her appointed times ..." Yet clearly ancient man did not know, nor for that matter does modern man. He does not believe that he is answerable to God, nor that his day of reckoning is coming when his whole past life will be judged by God. For the verse continues, "The turtle and the crane and the swallow observe the time of their coming, but my people know not the judgment of the Lord" [14]. How much the physical heavens and the natural world have to teach us!

LOOK TOWARD HEAVEN

In our day again, we are told by the cynics and critics that not only is God dead, but the whole idea of the institutional church will be wound up by the end of the twentieth century. They ask how can we expect any sensible person in the space age to believe in God. If statements like that get to you, disturb you and begin to undermine your faith, take a walk, not to escape from reality, but to face it. Take one of these modern unbelievers with you! Just make sure the evening is clear and simply, **"Look now toward heaven and tell the stars if thou be able to number them?"** [15].

This same advice was given to a solitary Christian at the beginning of the history of the world and of the Church. That man was Abraham, the great father of the faith. Let us stand where he stood and look at the stars and realise there are millions who will yet believe in God. Let us today hear the same words from God concerning the future multiplication of His Church, that He spoke to Abraham long ago. He said to him, "So shall thy seed be" [15]. Let our response now be the same as his then, "And he believed in the Lord" [16]. Incredible though it may seem, in our dark age of indifference to God and unbelief, God still promises His Church "I will multiply thy seed as the stars of the heaven, and the sand which is upon the sea shore" [17].

The next time you see the stars shining in the firmament above you, remember there are millions who have already believed, or will yet believe in Christ. And the next time you stand upon the sand, remember each grain is one of God's people.

Scripture References

1. Psalm 19:1
2. Psalm 19:2
3. Genesis 1:1
4. Psalm 8:3-4
5. Isaiah 55:8-9
6. Isaiah 55:10
7. Isaiah 55:10
8. Job 37:7
9. Job 37:8
10. Job 37:6
11. Job 38:37
12. Matthew 5:45
13. Matthew 6:26
14. Jeremiah 8:7
15. Genesis 15:5
16. Genesis 15:6
17. Genesis 22:17

2

Heaven -Begins Now

Present day Christians need to realise that heaven does not begin at glorification, but at regerneration. Indeed it will give us a new approach to Evangelism. For Christ evangelism was to lead men beyond earthly things and tell him of 'heavenly things', in order that he might really believe in them whilst still on earth. It changes the very encounter of God and man into a heavenly one and not merely an earthly one. This is particularly evident when we trace again the meeting between Christ and Nicodemus nearly two thousand years ago. He was one of the religious leaders of his day. Perhaps he was a coward because he came under cover of darkness. Yet, he clearly came as a seeker, like many before him and many since. A day or two before some of the thousands of Jews who crammed into Jerusalem for the Passover, had witnessed Christ performing miracles and, because through want they had seen, they believed in His name, Christ did not commit Himself to them, "Because he knew what was in man" [1]. Then, dramatically, John's Gospel declares, "There was a man ..."[2], and that man was Nicodemus - a kind of man who appears from nowhere. Yet he represents many who have come to Christ since. Now, confronted by Christ. Nicodemus says all the right things. He appears to play his hand well, acknowleged Christ to be a miracle worker, teacher and a man come from God. Yet, Christ read him like an open book (as, incidentally He does with every seeking soul). In one stroke He cuts through Niciodemus' religion and orthodoxy by answering the unspoken question in his heart with these words, "Verily, verily I say unto you, except a man be born again he cannot see the Kingdom of God" [2]. Literally He said, man must be born from above before he can become a Christian and enter the Kingdom of God. Heaven must begin here.

THE RUNAWAY

How interested heaven is in the salvation of a soul! We need to see that sin is against God and against heaven. Man is a runaway who needs to return to God in repentance and confess as did the prodigal of old, "I will arise and go to my Father and will say unto him, Father I have sinned against heaven and before thee," [3] or in the lovely words of Christina Rossetti's poem, 'A Prodigal Son'-

> "Fallen from sonship
> beggared of grace,
> Grant me my Father,
> a servant's place"

The greatest comfort is that the Father God Himself comes out of heaven to receive him back, for we read, "When he was a great way off, his father saw him and ran and fell on his neck and kissed him' [3]. And we are told that at that moment "Joy shall be in heaven over one sinner that repenteth, more than over ninety-and-nine just persons who need no repentance" [4].

HEAVENLY BIRTH

From the day when a man is born again, he comes to see things differently. He has to understand the sheer necessity of experiencieng a heavenly birth, because Christ said that without it, a man cannot see God's kingdom. By 'see' He meant perceive, know or comprehend that Kingdom, which is heaven above and also here below. It is to realise that without the Spirit of God, man is shut in upon himself, living in a purely human and earthly realm and incapable, therefore, of knowing God. It is like trying to speak to a foreigner, without knowing a word of his language, whereas, people of this world, because of their common humanity, can perfectly share earthly concerns. God puts it together so clearly when He says, "For what man knoweth the things of a man, save the spirit of man which is in him" [5]. The link is that two human beings have a like human spirit. You do not get the same response between man and any other animal, only human with human, but when man meets the divine, there is no such rapport. He has no means of communication, because he is devoid of the Spirit of God. That is why he needs to make contact with the divine. Before that it has to be reluctantly admitted that "the natural man receiveth not the things of the Spirit of God, for they are foolishness unto him, neither can he know them, because they are spiritually discerned" [5]. Man must come to see "Even so the things of God knoweth no man, but the Spirit of God" [5]. When He puts the Holy Spirit into our lives, we come not only to believe, but also to understand these words, "now we have received not the spirit of the world, but the Spirit which is of God" [5]. No man in this world will ever get into heaven, or enter into that new realm of living until he sees man for whom he is and God for whom He is. Christ states categorically that there are two births; we have all experienced one, and we must all experience two if we are to know God and heaven. In a word, Christ said, "That which is born of the flesh is flesh, and that which is born of the Spirit is Spirit" [6].

Every man needs to stand where Nicodemus stood long ago the night when he came to Christ. We are not born Christians. If he finds the idea of being born again incredible, he is in good company. For clearly Christ detected in the face of Nicodemus an expression of amazement and incredulity. Hence He addressed that and the unbelief behind it, when He said, "Marvel not that I said unto thee, ye must be born again." [6]

Whether the two of them were talking on the flat roof of the house in Jerusalem, or looking out through the open door or windows, suddenly the wind blew moving the palm trees nearby. Christ drew Nicodemus' attention to it, to elucidate the work of God's Holy Spirit and, in explanation, He said, "the wind bloweth where it listeth (chooses) and thou hearest the sound thereof, but canst not tell whence it cometh, or whither it goeth, so is everyone that is born of the Spirit". [6] No one has ever seen the wind, only the effects of it, as it moves the branches of the trees, so, though nobody has seen the wind of God's Spirit blowing from heaven, you can see the results of it in changed lives. Nicodemus, like many before and after him, took a lot of convincing, "How can these things be?"[6], he retorted. As a religious leader, Christ clearly thought such a theologian should have known better than that. "Art thou a master in Israel and knoweth not these things?" [6] flashed back the question in reply. Christ is telling Nicodemus that he is daring to call in question the evidence of his own eyes.

HEAVENLY THINGS

Up till now Christ has merely talked of earthly things, such as the movement of the wind, and even the meaning of that has been doubted. Christ clearly wants to take man further and introduce him to heavenly things, even whilst he is living in this present world. As much as to Nicodemus in his far off and forgotten day, Christ wants modern man to know and believe certain heavenly things. He must begin to see that even the commencement of Christianity and his being born again, takes him immediately beyond the things of earth. As we have seen a Christian is a person who has experienced being born from above. He is by sheer definition a man with two birthdays. That is how heaven begins here. Yet it would end here, if someone had not come from heaven, with the aim of taking us there one day.

One of the declared reasons for writing this book as stated in the preface, was to ask how can man get to heaven? Well, Christ's immediate answer is "No man hath ascended up to heaven, but he that came down from heaven, even the Son of Man which is in heaven". [6] With these words Jesus reveals Himself to us, not only as the heavenly Man, alias the Son of Man, but the one who has descended from heaven itself. Incidentally, He describes heaven as the place no man ascends to unassisted.

LIVING IN TWO WORLDS

In our twentieth century evangelism, we need to declare Christ, as not only God, but the unique man who has the ability to live in two worlds at the same time. Even as He spoke to Nicodemus, He was on earth and also in heaven. He could refer to Himself in one breath as both coming from heaven and being in heaven. Beyond this, He could not only be in two places at the same time, but also with two people simultaneously, one on earth and one in heaven. In the prologue of John's authentic Gospel and biography of Jesus Christ, He is described whilst on earth as also "The only begotten son which is in the bosom of the Father". [7]

On another occasion, Christ showed the vast gulf that existed between Him and any other man without the Spirit of God in these words, "Ye are **from beneath**; I am **from above**". [8]

The second great thing, to which Christ would introduce man, by his being born of God, is His heavenly work - His crucifixion. Someone may rightly say it was very much an earthly work which took place on that hill called Calvary, when for us sinners Christ literally bedewed the earth with His shed blood. That is unquestionably true, as far as it goes. Even here, in John's Gospel, Christ compares His death to that time in the history of God's ancient people, the Jews, when they were bitten by poisonous snakes and were therefore certainly going to die. But God commanded their leader, Moses, to make a brazen serpent, put it on a pole, and lift it up in the sight of the dying. He urged them to look to that serpent, and, in looking, they would in some miraculous way be saved from death. Likewise, when Christ would be lifted up on the cross to die, those who, having been bitten by that "old serpent called the devil", [9] look to Him will be saved from sin. Much nearer to the time of the crucifixion, Christ described His forthcoming death in these words, "And I, if I be lifted up from the earth will draw all men unto me! This he said signifying by what death he should die". [10] Yet, before there was an earth, before there was a creature in it, let alone a sinner, there was a "Cross in heaven". God's Son was slain in heaven in the mind and plan of His Father, before He was slain on earth by wicked men. For God who knew the man He had created - Adam - would sin against Him, set Christ aside, and literally marked Him out as a Saviour whilst He was still in heaven. He is described by God as "The lamb slain from the foundation of the world". [11]

Peter, writing the first of his two letters to the early Christians suffering persecution under the Roman Emperor, Nero, could see the death of Christ as both a heavenly and as an earthly event. One in which a holy God took part, and also evil men, - "Forasmuch as ye know that ye were not redeemed with corruptible things as silver and gold ... but with the precious blood of Christ, as a lamb without blemish and without spot; who verily was foreordained before the foundation of the world, but was manifest in these last times for you; who, by him do believe in God that raised him from the dead and gave him glory; that your faith and hope might be in God". [12]

A WORLD OF LOVE

From the very moment perishing sinners look to Christ who was lifted up to die, they receive heavenly, that is "eternal life". By faith they have the life which, like God, has no beginning and no ending. That life flows to them from the everlasting love of God, described in the verse which Martin Luther called the Bible in miniature - "For God so loved the world that He gave His only begotten Son, that whosoever believeth in Him, should not perish, but have everlasting life". [13] Heaven is a world of love and of life, yet both may be experienced on this earth. This is the heavenly cargo which Christ brought to this world. He could not have put it more beautifully than when He uttered these words, "I am the living bread which came down from heaven; if any man eat this bread, he shall live for ever and the bread that I will give is my flesh, which I will give for the life of the world". [14] Yet it is hardly credible that heaven has sent such love and such life into the world in the person of Christ, when we see men failing almost to exist, let alone to live. In the midst of the violence and hatred at the end of this twentieth century, of men to men and mankind to God, it seems the world has blatantly rejected, or at best forgotten, just what heaven has to offer.

Did you know that way back in the last century, when the first missionaries to the people of the island of Tahiti, told of heaven's love and the offer of eternal life, how unforgettable was their response? When told that "God so loved that he gave ...", they said, "Why have you been so long in coming, and how can you tell us without tears?" We seem to live in a world which has not only lost touch with heavenly things in the person of Christ, His sacrifice, His life and His love, but has also forgotten how to weep. It has forgotten, not only that Christ came, but from where He came and for what purpose. Life for millions has no earthly purpose, because they are largely ignorant of Christ's heavenly reason for coming to this world, which was solely one of salvation and not of condemnation. "For God sent not His son into the world to condemn the world, but that the world through Him might be saved". [15]

Yet, generally speaking, man has chosen the way of unbelief and lies in God's sight already condemned. The day of judgment will in fact be no more than the sentence already passed and, in a word, unbelieving man is already in the condemned cell under eternal life sentence.

TWENTIETH CENTURY DARKNESS

Not only is modern man, as much as the ancients, locked up in his own wilful unbelief, but, even worse, he is in a crisis situation, that is a spiritual crisis - a twentieth century dark ages. Christ describes this in these words "And this is the condemnation that light is come into the world, and men loved darkness rather than light". [15] If modern man asks the reason for the spiritual and moral crisis in our land, the answer in a word is that men have loved darkness rather than light. The bare reality and the fearful fact of fallen humanity will not just go away; it must be faced. Is it not "Everyone that doeth evil hateth light, neither cometh to the light". [15] There are those in our present world who are looking for "more light". They believe the dawning of another century will bring a new solution to all man's problems. To such people God and heaven have no light to throw. On the contrary, it is not that sufficient enlightenment on the subject has not been given from heaven, but man does not want it to discover the darkness of his life. He does not want to be found out. Christ sums it up when He says that man hates and will not come to the light "lest his deeds should be reproved" [15] (discovered - seen for what they are in broad daylight.)

Even the physical world was in darkness until God spoke from heaven and said "Let there be light and there was light". [16] So, even more, in the spiritual world the simple truth is "but if our gospel be hid, it is hid to them that are lost: In whom the god of this world hath blinded the minds of them that believe not, lest the light of the glorious gospel of Christ, who is the image of God should shine unto them". [17] Yet, once a man turns to the truth of God, he is unafraid of the light of God shining upon his life; in fact he has come to the one who said "I am the light of the world; he that followeth me shall not walk in darkness, but shall have the light of life". [18]

RISEN WITH CHRIST

Never was there a day in which we need to emphasise that every true Christian has experienced not only a new birth, but a spiritual resurrection, which has raised him to heaven. We have to stop and realise what condition we were in in God's sight before He put new life into us. In a word, He says we were "dead". A Christian is one who is back from the dead. God plainly states what He has done to us, "And you hath He quickened who were dead in trespasses and sins". [19] This explains why we were so apathetic, bored, indifferent and even antagonistic to the need of salvation. Sin has had a deadening effect on our lives. We were dead in a spiritual sense in the sphere of trespass, which is to break the law of God, whereas the word "sin" carries a military meaning in that God says "All have sinned and come short of the glory of God". [20] Our sights have been too low. The meaning of coming short carries the idea of the arc that the trajectory of the shell or missile makes. And we have by sin missed God's target - God Himself, His glory, that is His beauty, His wonder - the sum of all His perfections.

NEW DIMENSION OF LIVING

Before Christ came to us, we were like corpses lying in a grave, spiritually dead to God. The Apostle Paul was clearly convinced that even the early Christians were largely blind to the heavenly life to which God had lifted them. He was so disturbed that for a moment he put down his pen, as he was writing a letter to them, and prayed, that "The eyes of their understanding (heart) being enlightened that ye may know ... what is the exceeding greatness of his power to us-ward who believe, according to the working of His mighty power, which He wrought in Christ when He raised Him from the dead and set Him at His own right hand in heavenly places".[1] He is in fact saying that the same miraculous power which raised Christ's body physically from the grave on the third day and later into heaven, is the identical power that raises a Christian to spiritual life. This is the irrefutable proof, if you follow the divine logic. Our eyes must be opened to see that the same power has worked in the Christian, as earlier worked in Christ.

Secondly, it has performed the same work, in that, whereas Christ has been raised to physical life, we have been raised from spiritual darkness to spiritual life.

Thirdly, and perhaps most amazingly, the same power has raised Christ and the Christian to heaven, for Christ physically and for the true Christian spiritually, - His a physical resurrection, ours a spiritual. And, because of this, we are both in heaven this very day. We can do no better than show that, due to the richness of God's love and mercy, He has lifted us up to a new dimension of living.

No wonder Paul had to pray for the Christians of his day to grasp the wonder of it. Let God put it in His own words, "But God who is rich in mercy, for his great love wherewith he loved us, even when we were dead in sins, hath quickened us together with Christ (by grace are ye saved) and hath raised us up together and made us sit together in heavenly places in Christ Jesus ..." [22]

SEATED IN HEAVEN

It is clear now that it is no exaggeration to say heaven begins here - born from, raised to and seated in heaven with none other than Christ at God's right hand. What help and blessings can be received moment by moment down here if we only lived in the light of our heavenly life and position in Christ. This present world has nothing to give us in a spiritual sense. No wonder God says, "Blessed (literally God be praised or thanked) be the God and Father of our Lord Jesus Christ, who has blessed us with all spiritual blessings in **heavenly places in Christ**". [23] The Lord Jesus Himself has since His return to heaven reversed His position. For thirty-three yeas He lived in the body on earth and by the Spirit in heaven. Now, for nearly two thousand years He has lived in the body in heaven and by the Spirit on earth.

This is not meant to be a dull, boring, academic theological thesis, but a dynamic new dimension of life style possible in today's world. In a word, the source of our life is with God in heaven. No wonder Paul reminded the Philippian Christians living under the pagan Roman powers, no doubt as a great encouragement and inspiration to them, "For our conversation (way of life - life-style) is in heaven, from whence also we look for the Saviour, the Lord Jesus Christ, who shall change our vile body, that it may be fashioned like unto his glorious body, according to the working whereby He is able to subdue all things to Himself". [24] In down to earth practical living, it makes us take a new look at our priorities and possessions in the light of heaven. The words of Christ begin to carry devastating meaning for us today, locked up in our neat, modernistic, plastic world. Christ put His finger on the true pulse of our lives, painful though it may initially be, when He commanded us, "Lay not up for yourselves treasures upon earth, where moth and rust doth corrupt and where thieves break through and steal; but lay up for yourselves treasures in heaven where neither moth nor rust doth corrupt, and where thieves do not break through and steal". [25] Then He made perhaps His most telling point, when He concluded with these words, "For where your treasure is, there will your heart be also". [25] Surely, Paul's God-inspired words for truly successful living whilst here upon earth cannot be improved! "But godliness with contentment is great gain. For we brought nothing into this world and it is certain we can carry nothing out. And having food and raiment let us be therewith content. But they that be rich fall into temptation and a snare and into many foolish and hurtful lusts which drown men in destruction and perdition. For the love of money is the root of all evil: which while some have coveted after, they have erred from the faith, and pierced themselves through with many sorrows". [26]

When these heavenly things begin truly to dawn on the heart and mind, it is no exaggeration to say that life will never be quite the same again. It leads to a new outlook, to a new view of this world and of the world to come. It cannot be put better than the Apostle Paul did to the Christians living in the sea-port town of Corinth in Greece. It is important to notice that Corinth had been a byword for everything permissive. But since their conversion to Christ, Paul had encouraged the believers to see themselves on the one hand as dying physically, but having an inward life which could be daily renewed by God in such a way that they would begin to see the things of earth in the perspective of eternity and heaven. As he wrote his last letter to them, he includes himself in his advice, because he needs to maintain his own vision. So he writes, "For this cause **we** faint not, though our outward man perish, yet the inward man is renewed day by day. For our light affliction which is but for a moment, worketh for us a far more exceeding and eternal weight of glory; **while we look** not at the things which are seen, but at the things which are not seen: for the things which are seen are temporal, but the things which are not seen are eternal". [27]

VIEW OF HEAVEN

A view of heaven is immensely practical and realistic, in that we see these human bodies for what they really are; daily dying. But the life of God within us enables us to cope with the burdens and problems which are our constant companions in this life. How modern man needs to see this. We need to take out our scales and weigh the woes of this world by that of the glory to come. Our trials and sorrows seem unbearable until we put the weight of heaven in the other scale. Then suddenly they become light in comparison with the joys of eternity. Again, measure the duration of troubles in this life against the endless life to come and incredibly they are "but for a moment". I am convinced, that though there is certainly such a thing as mental illness, the wards of our hospitals would be much emptier if man only lived on earth in this way. Perhaps someone even contemplates taking his own life! Then follow another piece of Paul's advice, this time offered to people living under the very cruel government of Imperial Rome. He makes again an evaluation of earthly suffering in the light of heaven ahead "For I reckon" he judged "that the sufferings of this present time are not worthy to be compared with the glory which shall be revealed in us". [28] What a thought, that heaven would be incomplete in a sense, without every suffering believer down here. Truly, it has been said "Heaven will make amends for all". We shall see later in this book as we look into heaven itself, that it is a place of perfect and sublime happiness. It was this perspective that brought Christ through the agony of Calvary. For we are told that it was the anticipation of the joy to come that enabled Him to endure everything that was meted out to Him on the cross. What amazing words indeed are these, "Looking unto Jesus, the author and finisher of our faith, who for the joy that was set before him endured the cross, despising the shame, and is set down on the right hand of the throne of God". [29] To survey the suffering Saviour's gaze set on the joy of heaven before Him is essential :Lest ye be weary and faint in your minds". [29]

Man must be brought to the point of decision, namely, whether to continue to live for this present world, or to begin to live for the one to come. The simple difference between heaven and earth in this life, centres upon one word alone "If" - It is a far more vital "If" than Rudyard Kipling's. It will not only bring him in a totally different direction here below, but new desires also. Paul wants to show the practical outworking of being spiritually lifted to heaven when he writes, "If ye be risen with Christ, seek those things which are above, where Christ sitteth on the right hand of God". [30]

A NEW TREASURE

We then begin to direct our lives towards heaven where not only Christ is, but where we are too. No longer do things on earth satisfy us as they used to do. We seek Christ's peace, power, love, happiness and presence above everything else and anyone else. It literally brings a new driving force to our lives, which directs us constantly heavenward. Paul puts it like this, "For the love of Christ constrains (drives) us, because we thus judge that if One died for all, then were all dead: And that He died for all, that they which live should not henceforth live unto themselves, but unto Him which died for them and rose again." [31] We no longer live solely for ourselves, but for the One who has died for us and has risen again, not only to give us the gift of His resurrection life, but has taken us with Him to heaven. Christ and heaven have "stolen" our hearts away, in that we "set our affections on things above, not on things on earth", [32] because we have found new treasure in the things of God, which makes the passing enjoyments on earth tinsel in comparison.

The old ego, the old ruling selfish I in our lives has been crucified with Christ on the cross, so that Paul can say of every true heaven seeking and loving Christian, "for ye are dead". [32] By faith we have become united with Christ's crucifixion, in that He died for our sins in order that we might know self-crucifixion in our lives. As Paul puts it so powerfully elsewhere, "I am crucified with Christ, nevertheless I live, yet not I, but Christ liveth in me, and the life which I now live, I live by the faith of the Son of God, who loved me and gave Himself for me". [33]

Yes, we are now vitally connected with the heavenly life of God. Though every person who is a Christian is, of course, a separate entity from Christ, he shares the same life. In this world Christ lives in him. Christ is as much alive in a Christian in New York or Paris, as he was alive in His body nearly two thousand years ago in Jerusalem. He wants to live "again" in you and me. But sometimes we simply feel we have not got the power to let Christ live like that in us in this tough old world. We forget that we now have a hidden life, which finds its source in Christ Himself. It is to see that our true life is above - for Paul would this day direct us to a new dimension of living - "Your life is hid with Christ in God". [34] What is seen and heard on earth is but our expressions, actions and words, but they flow from the unseen source above. We literally live out Christ's life in this twentieth century world. We shall do so until the day when the Lord shall come for us and take us to glory to be with Him for ever. No wonder it says that this will happen "When Christ who is our life shall appear". He truly is coming back to this world sooner than we think. His purpose for the Christian is that "then shall ye also appear with Him in glory". [34]

MOMENTOUS COMING EVENT

Such a momentous coming event for us all should lead to a radical change in our life-style on earth in the light of heaven, that is the end of the world and the coming back of God's Son. In a word Paul says, "Mortify (kill, throttle by the power of Christ's victorious death over sin) your members which are upon the earth". [34] Those lusts and passions in all of us by nature, can destroy us and prevent our ever getting to heaven, that is our sinful ways, such as "fornication (immorality), uncleanness (impurity), inordinate affection (passion), evil concupiscence (evil desire) and covetousness which is idolatry". [34]

We should not only crucify them with the power of Christ's sin-conquering life, but realise that at the end of the world God's wrath will fall upon such lives that have not given up on these things, for they will shut us out of heaven. That wrath, if we did but lift up our eyes, hangs over us like an unmoving relentless cloud. For Christ very definitely declared in His lifetime, 'He that believeth on the Son of God hath everlasting life: and he that believeth not the Son shall not see life: but the wrath of God abideth on him". [35]

That wrath or holy and righteous anger against our sins must be faced up to. The very sins which unrepented of here will not only shut us out of heaven, but will be punished **from** heaven. God's wrath does not derive its origin from hell, but from heaven, which is not only a place of love, but of holy and pure justice. "For the wrath of God is revealed **from heaven** against all ungodliness and unrighteousness of men, who hold (literally seek to suppress - hold down) the truth in unrighteousness". [36] Thank God, that as a godly Scotsman once said "Love warns". Let us all the more, therefore, continue our pursuit of heaven, our rightful home and, at the same time, shun everything that would seek to harm and hinder our heavenward climb.

Scripture References

1. John 2: 25
2. John 3: 1-3
3. Luke 15: 18-20
4. Luke 15: 7
5. 1 Cor. 2: 11-14
6. John 3: 6-13
7. John 1: 18
8. John 8: 23
9. Rev. 12: 9
10. John 12: 32-33
11. Rev. 13: 8
12. 1 Pet. 1: 18-21
13. John 3: 15-16
14. John 6: 51
15. John 3: 17-20
16. Gen. 1: 3

17. 2 Cor. 4: 3-4
18. John 8: 12
19. Eph. 2: 1
20. Rom. 3: 23
21. Eph 1: 18-20
22. Eph. 2: 4-6
23. Eph 1: 3
24. Phil 3: 20-21
25. Matt. 6: 19-21
26. 1 Tim. 6: 7-10
27. 2 Cor. 4: 18
28. Rom. 8: 18
29. Heb. 12: 2-3
30. Col. 3: 1
31. 2 Cor. 5: 14
32. Col. 3: 2-3
33. Gal. 2: 20
34. Col. 3: 3-5
35. John 3: 36
36. Rom. 1: 18

3

Heaven
-The Home of God

Heaven is the place which is too small for God, "... seeing the heaven of heavens cannot contain him".[1] In a sense God has a kind of housing problem. This was the discovery of the man who set out to build the largest place of worship on earth, in an attempt to localise God. Yet you cannot lock up the Most High in His world. For this reason Solomon was forced to exclaim, "Who is able to build Him a house?"[1] The being of God overflows from heaven above and spills over to fill this earth below, and we are forced to draw the amazing conclusion that "The Lord is God of heaven above and upon the earth beneath; there is none else".[2]

HIGHEST ALTITUDE

Yet heaven is still God's home, the place where He chooses to live. Heaven is the place of highest altitude, which comes to us as a self-revelation of God, "For thus saith the high and lofty One ... I dwell in the high place".[3] Heaven is named after God and it is therefore holy in character. This means it is not only a place of perfect purity; it is germ free, grave free and sin free. It is separated from the whole creation spreading out beneath it, and from every creature populating the so-called planet earth. "God's "Name is holy"[3] and, therefore, He lives in an environment conducive to His person. He simply states "I dwell in the holy place"[3] - this is God's address above. Yet, He has another address below. The God of heaven sets up His home in the lowly back street called Man - a broken hearted and lowly man, conscious of his sinfulness and shame. This is where God moves into and lives on earth. The American - Tozer - put it perfectly when he described "Man the dwelling place of God". Oh! that modern twentieth century man realised that God wants to put heaven in our hearts. It is only our pride and high-mindedness that shuts God and heaven out. The sole condition of His entry is that we be characterised by a "contrite and humble spirit".[3] God further promises "to revive" such a heart with the breath of His own heavenly life and Spirit.

God also lives in timelessness, a place without beginning or end; in a world without a clock and without a calendar. He lives in the eternal now. He is the "One that inhabiteth eternity".

Beyond this we need to see heaven as a Royal Palace, where the King of Kings reigns, and from where He rules heaven and earth. He therefore informs us that "The heaven is my throne and the earth is my footstool".[4]

There is meant to be a constant traffic between man on earth and God in heaven. For another amazing fact is that earth can be seen from heaven. That means that our lives are not hidden from God, as man seems to think by the way he lives. Men of old used to ask God to look upon His world and particularly upon the plight and problems of man. He clearly felt that only heaven had the answer to his dilemma on earth. So he would pray to God like this, "Look down from heaven, from the habitation of Thy holiness and of Thy glory; where is Thy zeal and Thy strength, the sounding of Thy bowels (depths) and of Thy mercies toward me? Are they restrained?"[5] Man believed heaven had a heart which cared for him in his sin. God's mercy was the answer to man's misery and the cure of the mess he had made of his world.

He believed that God was not too busy with the running of His world to make time to guide each individual man's life, as he trusted in God and reposed faith in Christ as Saviour, his faith resting in a God who would guide him through the maze of this world and then one day receive him to glory above. He would address himself often to heaven in the midst of life, wherever he was and whatever his condition and simply declare "Thou wilt guide me with thy counsel and afterward receive me to glory".[6]

Man did not seem to need at his beck and call as modern people do, a troop of philosophers, psychiatrists, mediums, fortune tellers and social workers to tell him how to live in this welfare state. God was man's sole guide and counsellor through all the ups and downs of life. He knew heaven had a heart and a mind flowing freely with mercy and wisdom. For this reason no doubt, God became to such people the most desirable person in heaven and upon earth. Man knew he could look up and find God surveying his scene on earth; the street where he lived and where his children played, also the place where he worked. He had a father in heaven. It was the most desirable place, where the most desirable person lived and like Dr. Barnardo's, God's door was never shut. Man unashamedly confessed "Whom I have in heaven but thee ... and there is none on earth I desire beside thee". [6]

Oh! that we modern people shut in our technological world would learn today the desirableness of heaven and re-open communication with it. For we can still receive news from heaven. It has surely never been so beautifully described as "Good news from a far country".[7] We are not cut off. In the same way that Jacob saw a ladder between heaven and earth and the angels of God ascending and descending upon it",[8] we can now know that Christ is our ladder to heaven.

Sometimes through our Bibles (though written thousands of years ago) we get a word coming personally from God. It is not something we deduce through simply sitting down with the Scriptures. Rather it is a word coming directly from heaven to our hearts, speaking as plainly and as powerfully as an audible voice to us individually, as if we were the only ones in the world. It is carried speedily on the cable of the Holy Spirit from God's home to ours. It brings God's news into our little world, our bedroom, our kitchen, our lounge, and everything is different from that moment. It is much more than God's voice speaking through the Bible to us today., It is certainly that, but beyond that it is God Himself coming from heaven. It is the fulfilment of His promise "I will come to you".[10] Like the apostles of old we can equally say, "Truly our fellowship (togetherness) is with the Father and with His Son Jesus Christ".[11] By the Spirit of God He still comes and holds a conversation with us as intimately and as personally as he did with Abraham in the plains of Mamre".[12]

LIGHT OF THE WORLD

Have you ever seen that amazing painting of Holman Hunt's with Christ as the light of the world, standing outside a door with His lamp in His hand? His face is grave and sad, for it is apparent the door has not been opened for a very long time, being overgrown with weeds. The door represents the human heart closed to the God of heaven. It is not only the door of the world, but also of the Church. It is not merely an artist's impression, but portrays Jesus Christ writing a letter from heaven to a particular church on earth. He is saying in so many words, "I am not content to write to you (in My word - the Bible), but I want to come from heaven and live within you"."Behold I stand at the door and knock. If any man hear my voice and open the door, I will come in".[13] Christ is knocking with His heavenly knuckles on the door of our hearts. He wants to live intimately with us and dine with us as personally as He sat at the table of Mary, Martha and Lazarus in Bethany, ate their food and shared their lives.[14] That is where heaven begins - here.

THE NIGHT VISITOR

When a person is alone in a room at night, when others have all gone to bed, it is possible to receive a visit from that far country in the form of a night visitor, like David of old in the Bible when he said, "Thou hast visited me in the night".[15] There was a little boy in hospital. He dreaded his mother leaving him, for he was facing an operation next day. But his pastor told him, "When mummy has gone, the night visitor will come, even though it is after visiting hours". The Lord Jesus he was told would walk into his ward that night. Cheered, he willingly let his mother go, so keen was he for the night visitor to come, and he was not disappointed. It is a truly wonderful thing to be on visiting terms with God and to know visits from heaven.

Hourly also, heaven listens to earth's news. In fact among many of God's books, there is "the book of remembrance", in which are recorded all the communications between God-fearing men and women about Christ here on earth. It records not only their words about Him, but even their thoughts also. In some amazing way, God literally hears the voices of men and women about Him in this world. What a tremendous thought! It is reported by God, "Then they that feared the Lord spoke often one to another and the Lord hearkened and heard it, and a book of remembrance was written before Him for them that feared the Lord and thought upon His name".[16] Such people are precious to God. That is not too strong a description of them. In pre-dating heaven, God says of them "They shall be mine in the day when I make up my jewels (special treasure)".[16] That day is the end of the world, which will herald in the endless day of heaven. Such people God will set as gems is His crown and promises to treat them as "His own Son". [16 B]

It is evident that God keeps an account of all our movements here on earth from the first day we believe on Him, until He takes us up to heaven. For when a person believes in this world, in some incredible way, that event is news above. For we are told, "There is joy in the presence of the angels over one sinner that repenteth". [17]

Perhaps we should not be surprised that heaven knows about us, because it knew about Christ and followed His life on earth for something like thirty-three years.

SOLITARY ANGEL

What must that solitary angel have thought as it flew on its heavenly mission to the fields of Bethlehem? Did it not expect millions to be lining the route, anxious to catch a glimpse of the newly-born babe? Would not every eye look up into the starry sky to hear the angel's message from God? Yet, what disappointment must have filled that angel's heart, as it saw the empty fields, save for a few shepherds on the night shift watching over their flocks of sheep, and anyway, they would not be interested. They would be far too busy to have any time for God. The angel flew lower and lower till he literally "came upon them".[18] The angel saw their brown weather-beaten faces, suddenly awestruck and filled with fear, particularly as the burning pure light of heavenly glory lit up the fields of Bethlehem, as if it were mid day. Through the angel heaven spoke, "Fear not, for I bring you good tidings, which shall be to all people".[18]

Here was the best news ever to come from heaven and yet there was only a handful to hear it. But such indifference never silenced heaven's voice then, nor thankfully, ever since. The angel must speak God's only message of hope to the world, "For unto you is born this day in the city of David a Saviour, which is Christ the Lord".[18]

Heaven's news that first Christmas and ever since is that the Saviour has come to bring joy to the world - the joy of sins forgiven through that coming. Suddenly the greatest choir ever heard broke the silence of the night air. The heavenly angels could contain themselves not a moment longer. "And there was with the angels a multitude of the heavenly host praising God and saying 'Glory to God in the highest and on earth peace and goodwill towards men'".[18] What a moment of history that was! Sinless angels singing over Christ's birthplace, whilst sinful men for whom He came had "no room"[19] for heaven's gift that first Christmas. Yet that visitation did not go totally unheeded, in that we read, "and it came to pass as the angels were gone away into heaven, the shepherds said one to the other, 'Let us go even now unto Bethlehem ...'".[20]

No doubt heaven continued to follow the Christ, with angelic instructions to Joseph to take the young child to Egypt and later to return to Israel and God Himself telling Joseph in a dream to go into Galilee, thus following His life through the village school and into his father's carpenter's shop, until the moment when He stood praying with the waters of the Jordan rolling at His feet on the day of His baptism. Suddenly heaven was literally ripped open above Him, like a torn piece of cloth. Then through the rent skies, the Spirit of God flew down in the bodily form of a dove. And, through that "hole" in heaven, there followed the Father's voice saying, "Thou art my beloved Son; in thee I am well pleased". [21]

Oh! that every true Christian today deduced from this that God in heaven equally follows the steps of His twentieth century sons and daughters in this same world. He often draws back the curtains of heaven and surveys our earthly lot. He still sends His Spirit to anoint our dry lives and, as we have already noticed, speaks through the voice of Scripture to assure us that our lives on earth can still bring pleasure and happiness to His heart in heaven. Yet there were not only recorded Christ's red letter days in this world, like His baptism, but also the dark days of trials, temptations and assaults of the devil in His wilderness experience. For forty days heaven witnessed every taunt and acidic accusation flung at His flawless life. Then the Father sent to His rescue in the form of the angels who came and ministered to His need".[22]

Now three years have flown. The time - dead of night, the location - a garden of olive trees, with eight men at a distance from the central figure. But sleep has overtaken them and they are now oblivious to His presence. Three other forms about a stone's cast from the lonely Christ lie in a similar state, for sleep has got the better of them too. The solitary figure is bent in prayer, then at times He goes to His friends, but, finding no help from their sleeping forms, returns to His place again. Falling upon His knees, He fills the night air with His prayers, which sound more like cries. This is His final battle with His satanic foe who has dogged His every step for thirty-three years. His human form would rather find a way out, if that were possible, from the ultimate fight unto death, within hours to be fought on a nearby hill called Calvary. Heaven will witness that also. But returning to the garden scene, He uttered His final prayer, which flies like a gun-shot to heaven - "Father, if thou be willing remove this cup from me; nevertheless, not my will but thine be done". [22a]

For a moment heaven is silent, no rending of the skies breaks the night air, no form of a dove rests upon His sweating brow, no pleasing voice of His Father reassures Him all is well. Only silence! Then He senses someone is coming to His aid. Then, "There appeared an angel unto Him from heaven". [22a] Not this time a singing angel (for this is no time for singing) but a strengthening angel to fortify His failing human form, as at His temptation. The result of heaven's intervention is that He throws Himself again into the spiritual warfare, "Not against flesh and blood, but against principalities and powers, against the rulers of the darkness of this world, against spiritual wickedness in high places". [23] Now heaven witnesses the nearly inhuman intensity of His combat with the devil, for Christ, "Being in an agony prayed the more earnestly". [24] He was strengthened by heaven to pray to heaven to overcome diabolos. Suddenly, the very vessels in His brow break under the fearful tension, "And His sweat was as it were great drops of blood falling down to the ground". [24] The cost of His victory is nothing less than His blood bedewing the earth upon which, only a few yards away His disciples are "sleeping for sorrow". [24]

Let us never forget heaven also viewed the crucifixion. Here it is evident that earth is aware of heaven as, equally, heaven is of earth. The first act of Christ upon the cross is to address God. "Then said, Jesus 'Father, forgive them, for they know not what they do'". [25]

As the events of agony move on, it is clear that Christ's communion with heaven is amazingly dawning upon the darkened minds of one of the guilty criminals crucified beside Him. He is brought to realise, not only that Christ is innocent, whereas he and his companion are guilty, but that a King is being crucified alongside him - one who has a Father in heaven, and a Kingdom awaiting Him there. He clearly realises that this is Christ, the chosen of God. Now it is the criminal's turn to pray and he beseeches the God beside him to take him to His heavenly kingdom above. This is a model prayer for any sinner reading this book today, who wants to be remembered by God, to know Jesus, the Saviour and Lord, and to be received by the King when He arrives in His heavenly Kingdom. Just listen to his prayer and the immediate answer he received. "He said unto Jesus, 'Lord remember me when thou comest into thy kingdom'". [26] As quickly as he prayed for the salvation of his soul and the certainly of heaven, Christ's answer flashed back - "Today shalt thou be with me in paradise". [26] Where Christ is, is Paradise - that is His kingdom - that is heaven.

THE SUN HID ITS FACE

Suddenly, even heaven had enough of all the hatred, cursing and mocking of Christ by the supposed ministers of religion surrounding the cross and their worked-up mob, who earlier had been programmed by them to shout repeatedly two words sufficient to seal His doom - "Crucify Him". [27] The sun in the sky, unnoticed by the rebels against God below, rose to its highest and hottest point on the stroke of midday. Suddenly, miraculously, "there was darkness over the whole earth". [28] This was no total eclipse of the sun as had been suggested by the critics of God, for Christ died at the time of the Passover, when it was always full moon, and such an eclipse impossible. This was one of heaven's miracles. For three hours the sun hid its light from the face of God, bleeding from its crown of embedded thorns and running with the horror of human spittle - a visage, though victorious indeed, was marred more than any man's. Even in far off Egypt, a pagan philosopher recorded the darkness and discerned that some deity was displaying its displeasure.

Then, finally, there broke from the Saviour's lips a cry of victory "Finished". [29] He handed back His life spirit to His Father in heaven, bowed His holy head and expired. At that very moment, "the veil of the temple was rent in the midst". [30] Not by any human hand, but rather by a heavenly one, tearing the thick and heavy curtain, which had hidden the glory of God from man. The rent was from God to man and from heaven to earth. At that moment, Christ presented His blood into heaven and from that moment also the door of heaven has been opened. [31]

"Who yielded His life an atonement for sin
And opened the life-gate that all may go in"

Scripture References

1. 2 Chron. 2: 6
2. Deut. 4: 39
3. Isaiah 57: 15
4. Isaiah 66: 1
5. Isaiah 63: 15
6. Psalm 73: 24, 25
7. Prov. 25: 25
8. Gen. 28: 12
9. John 1: 51
10. John 14: 18
11. 1 John 1: 3
12. Gen 18: 1
13. Rev. 3: 20
14. John 12: 2
15. Psalm 17: 3
16. Malachi 3: 16, 17
16B. Malachi 3:17
17. Luke 15: 7
18. Luke 2: 9-14
19. Luke 2: 7
20. Luke 2: 15-20
21. Luke 3: 22
22 Mark 1: 13
22a. Luke 22: 42, 43
23. Eph. 6: 12
24. Luke 22: 44, 45
25. Luke 23: 34
26. Luke 23: 42, 43
27. Luke 23: 21
28. Luke 23: 44, 45
29. John 19: 30
30. Luke 23: 45
31. Hebrews 10: 19

4

Heaven
– News from Below

The question is often asked, do people in heaven know what is going on on earth? It is not possible to answer with a categorical "No", nor for that matter with an absolute "Yes". But it cannot with certainty be ruled out that those in heaven do witness events on earth and watch a Christian's journey - his race towards heaven.

The writer to the Hebrews wanted to encourage those Christians of long ago who were finding the going hard. He does it by assuring them that they are surrounded by believers who have already reached heaven. He had just taken his readers through a meandering tour of God's great gallery of the spiritual giants of the past. The eleventh chapter of Hebrews brings its readers face to face with the portraits of the greatest men and women who ever lived in this world. Yet their eyes were always turned towards heaven. Their earthly accomplishments and their eventual arrival there, were due to one thing only - faith. An impressive arch marks the entrance to the gallery upon which is written the words of their life-long secret, "The just shall live by faith". [1] Faith was the veritable fuel of their lives, which drove them relentlessly onward, come what may. We must return later to one or two of these portraits and examine them more closely. But now let us turn to what is, perhaps, the sole statement in Scripture which gives us some evidence for thinking that the victors of faith are watching our progress.

OLYMPIC GAMES

With the purpose of increasing the competitors' speed and unrelenting resolve, the writer makes us look at those who are on God's victory rostrum, who have received their respective golds, silver or bronze medals. For a moment he makes us look away from the race we are running here below. He instructs us by such words as these, "Wherefore seeing we are compassed about by so great a cloud of witnesses".² The earthly winners have now been promoted to being heavenly witnesses, watching us competing in the same stadium, simply called earth. In fact we are running not only in the same arena in which they ran, but in the same race. It is apparently true that in the early Greek and Olympic games, there was a stand specially reserved for former champions, so they could watch the present athletes striving for trophies. They obviously were there, not only to watch, but also to cheer on those participating. It appears also that this stand for past champions was set behind the winning post, so that they could be seen by present competitors. both present and past, therefore, were aware of each other. But though heaven can see earth, earth can only see heaven by faith, and we are to be inspired heavenward solely by following "in the steps of that faith".³

One of the witnesses on the heavenly rostrum looking down upon us is a man named Enoch, who has left in God's book of records his secret - he "walked with God". ⁴ He never walked alone. When we consider the birth and background of Enoch, we find no fact of great interest. In fact the world knows more about his son Methuselah, than about Enoch. It does so because Methuselah lived nine hundred and sixty-nine years, the world being concerned with how long we live, but God is concerned with **how** we live. So the Bible reminds us of Enoch, whilst we do not know that Methuselah ever walked one day of his long life with God.

As we open the book of Genesis, we read "And Enoch walked with God after he begat Methuselah three hundred years". ⁴ It does not say that he had always done so, for there must come a day when a man begins his walk towards heaven. In tracing his genealogy, we find that he was the seventh from Adam, the first man in the world. ⁵ Alas, he bore not only the physical characteristics of Adam, but also the fallen ones. It is at this point indeed that all men commence their earthly life, for Enoch's plight is the same for all mankind. The Bible plainly states that when the first runner in the heavenly race - Adam - fell through disobedience, we were all involved in his handicap. His fall has impeded everyone since. It says "Wherefore as by one man sin entered into the world, and death by sin; and so death passed upon all men, for that all have sinned". ⁶ Enoch, like all men, began his life out of step with God. He could not do otherwise, "For two cannot walk together except they be agreed".[7] How then did he begin? The writer to the Hebrews answers our question when he says, "By faith Enoch ..." He learned that without faith, it is impossible to please God.

FAMOUS SCIENTIST

This reminds me of a woman I knew, near to the door of heaven, though she was finishing her days on earth in an old people's home. Her speech had almost gone; in fact it took her several minutes to form a whole sentence. One day when I visited her, I found her very agitated. At last she formed the words, "My son is a famous scientist", and finally she conveyed to me, not only by the words I so slowly drew out of her, but by her pained expression, that her son's scientific fame had been achieved at the cost of his former Christian faith. She arranged a meeting for us - an unforgettable occasion on a sunny Surrey evening. Her son and I, having both visited the dear lady, literally on the last lap of the race, walked together up the road. At the top of it I knew I must turn in one direction and the Professor in another. We talked on about his life and accomplishments in research. Suddenly he spun round on me and said, "What about the moon? What about the people on the moon?" "Well", I answered, we don't know whether there is anyone on the moon, but if there is, Christ died for them too, because it is still God's world". We walked on in silence. Our point of departure from one another neared with every step. I felt how his mother was praying for him and particularly for me that I might draw him back to faith in God. This time I broke the silence, "Is there any place in your thinking for faith?", I asked him. "What do you mean?" he asked abruptly. I replied "God says, 'Without faith it is impossible to please him, for he that cometh to God must believe that He is, and that He is the rewarder of them that diligently seek him'".[8] "So what?" he retorted. "Well", I said, "If someone asked you to meet him at a certain place, provided you believed that person's word, and, of course, if you wanted to meet him, you would turn up wouldn't you?". "Yes" he replied hesitantly. "Well" I said, "It seems that you would turn up on the word of man, but not on the word of God!"

The Professor's reaction was one of the most incredible acts I ever saw from such a brilliant man. His right hand dived into his trouser pocket and immediately reappeared with a coin, which he held with precision between the index finger of his right hand and his thumb. Then, looking at me, he said in a staccato tone, "The time may come when I drop this coin and it will not fall but rise". I could not believe my ears and (looking back) I am convinced that God had so reached him, that for a moment he appeared to have lost his reason. I answered, "Before that can happen, God would have to change the law of gravity". The point of departure had been reached, and we parted, apparently never to meet again.

NOW IN HEAVEN

For some reason I was away from home for a few days and shortly after I returned the telephone rang. The voice was the Professor's, yet it sounded different. The arrogant atheistic voice could not be heard. A sad, flat voice, with all the confidence drained out of it said, "My mother is dead". I responded with genuine sympathy, to which he replied, "I tried to reach you, for I wanted you to take the funeral". I quietly answered, "You know your mother was a woman of great faith. She is now in heaven". "Yes, I know that" the atheist of yesterday replied. He thanked me for all I had done for her and then quickly rang off. I have inserted this story beside that of Enoch, because without faith it is still impossible to please God. When I see that man's face on the television screen, I wonder whether I shall see it in heaven. Has he made an appointment with God and found that He did turn up? Heaven alone will tell. Professors, Kings and Queens, politicians of whatever persuasion, or hawks and doves in Washington, must all learn to take the long road that Enoch took, not down the corridors of power in this world, but down the narrow road that leads to life and heaven.

ENOCH'S WALKING COMPANION

But the word "walked" describes not only the commencement of his godly life, but also the companionship that he now began to experience. He no longer journeyed alone through his earthly pilgrimage; he had a fellow traveller. He had the best company, because he had God. How many lives are ruined today, not because they have no companions, but because they have the wrong ones. Such can only lead astray and never to heaven.

As we take a last look at the life of this man Enoch, we notice that the word "walked" speaks of continuance, but how many we meet feel if they began the Christian life, they would never be able to keep it up. How wrong they are, for it was "with God" that Enoch walked. And He whispers a promise in our ears - "As thy days so shall thy strength be".⁹ Enoch did not go ahead of God, neither did he like Peter later, "follow afar off". No, for we read again, "And Enoch walked with God, and he was not for God took him". ¹⁰ "Oh" you might say as your eye passes from his life to his departure from this world, "What a strange end". But Enoch lived differently from other men, therefore his leaving this earth was different. The way we live, determines the way we die. If we live with God, we shall die with Him and go to be with Him. The writer to the Hebrews throws even more light on Enoch's passing when he writes, "By faith Enoch was translated, that he should not see death and was not found, because God had translated him". ¹¹ What reason had God for so amazingly transferring him from earth to heaven? That question too is answered. We read, "For before his translation he had this testimony that he pleased God". ¹¹

Enoch left no body to bury, no grave, no tombstone to be read by man. He left behind no testimonial on earth, but he had the highest in heaven - "He pleased God". It was the highest, for only of His Son did God say, "Thou art my beloved, in whom I am well pleased". ¹² As we too walk with God by faith, we too shall have that heavenly testimony when we come to pass from this earthly scene.

ABRAHAM'S MARCH NEARER HOME

I remind you that we are following the writer to the Hebrews injunction to take a close look at some of those in heaven, who are, in all probability, literally looking upon us at this very moment, as I am writing this book, and you, hopefully, will read it later. From Enoch we have seen how he walked with God from earth to heaven. An old Scottish divine said of him, "Enoch one day took a longer walk and did not come back". Only when we finish our journey, are we allowed to look down from heaven upon the same stadium where the athletes compete.

Let us now take a briefer look at another of the multitudes of former champions in the heavenly stand. Let us pick out this man - Abraham. What can we learn from him? Well, he is an example for us to follow in his steps to heaven. His message to us is simple - when God calls, go! Even if it appears a journey to nowhere. His life's secret is "By faith Abraham when he was called to go out to a place he should after receive for an inheritance obeyed; and he went out not knowing whither he went". [13] You see he simply rested by naked faith on the bare word of God. Oh! he found this world "A strange country". [13] He never put down his roots here. He never let them go deeper than his tent posts before he moved on, "A day's march nearer home". No wonder in heaven he has a grand-stand view of this still "strange country", where we exist today. He never would have looked for that cottage with roses round the door to which to retire and end his days, nor a modern castle in the "computer belt" world. For faith looks beyond the fading fabric of this earth. Beyond too, the fun-scene of this twentieth century vanity fair. We are commanded to look, not through man's rose-coloured spectacles, but through God's own long-sighted glasses and see heaven on a "clear day". "For he looked for a city which hath foundations, whose builder and maker is God". [13] No wonder we are commanded to be seeing daily by faith that "We are compassed about by so great a cloud of witnesses". [2] Everyone that we see upon that heavenly rostrum had given up hope of finding Utopia on earth. They have all "confessed that they were strangers and pilgrims on earth, for they that say such things declare plainly that they seek a country ... **that is a heavenly**, wherefore God is not ashamed to be called their God, for he hath prepared for them a city". [14]

Only God-given faith discovers that this world is doomed, has no foundations and is going nowhere. It has nothing that is lasting. It needs an old Chinese proverb stuck on all its contents - "This also will pass away" - I believe there must come a day in every person's life, when he sees that this world is ultimately worth nothing and from that day he beings to seek the lasting world of wonder - heaven. For me it happened when God led me to leave the first church of which I was pastor. I knew those hundred people better than anyone else. They were my family; their joys had been mine as were their sorrows. When they came to faith in God, their heaven became two heavens to me. It was my patch on which I was willing to stay till God called me, or came for me. Reluctantly I learned the hardest lesson, never I hope to have to learn again. It was simply this, "here we have no continuing city, but we seek one to come". [15]

> "Fading is the worlding's pleasure
> All his boasted pomp and show;
> Solid joys and lasting treasure
> None but Zion's children know."

The sight of such men as Enoch and Abraham upon that victory rostrum should be a source of great inspiration to us to run as they ran. We have also the added incentive that they are in all probability watching with bated breath our race to heaven. We are to learn from them to "Lay aside every weight" [2] and handicap of sin, which can so easily impede our progress. Oh! if we could only realise that our most mundane, as well as our intimate daily acts are viewed from heaven. It is most beautifully recorded in these poetic words:-

"To everything there is a season and a time to every purpose **under heaven**

A time to be born and a time to die, a time to plant and a time to pluck up that which is planted;

A time to kill and a time to heal; a time to break down and a time to build up

A time to cast away stones; a time to gather stones together;

A time to embrace and a time to refrain from embracing;

A time to get and a time to lose; a time to keep and a time to cast away;

A time to rend and a time to sew; a time to speak and a time to keep silence;

A time to love and a time to hate, a time of war and a time of peace". [16]

Incredibly heaven knows all! The life of every man on this earth is naked before God, and our most personal life is read from heaven like an open book. We are indeed told, "Neither is there any creature that is not manifest in his sight, but all things are naked and open unto the God with whom we have to do". [17]

The fact of our living before the all-seeing eye of God should lead us this moment up to the Christ who, "is passed into the heavens". [17] Yet His re-entry there from this world has not rendered Him insensitive to our feelings. Indeed He is "touched with the feeling of our infirmities", [17] particularly as He was "In all points tempted like as we are, yet without sin". [17] There is no need to wait a moment longer. Take your sin, your sorrow, your hurt, your care, immediately to God in prayer. The King of Kings invites us personally to "Come boldly unto the throne of grace, that we may obtain mercy and find grace to help in time of need". [17]

When a true believer comes to die, in the place where he draws his latest breath, heaven is there in a second and that person is carried by the angels to the home above. There is hardly a more vivid story in the Bible than that of a believing beggar being carried into heaven the moment he died, to be beside Abraham. Daily in every hospital ward, even if the doctors and nurses do not know it, they are brushing shoulders with angels on their way to carry believers into God's presence. Every death of a Christian is a newsflash immediately in heaven! We are indeed told "Precious in the sight of the Lord is the death of his saints". [18]

CONCERT PIANIST

These very words bring back to my mind the first death-bed to which I was called when I was a young minister. I visited a lady in her home when she was dying of cancer. Just as I was leaving, she quoted some beautiful words of a hymn, which she asked me did I know. I had to admit that I did not, but I was sure my wife would, and as soon as I reached home I would ask her. As I expected she was able to locate the hymn. That evening the lady's daughter rang me to say her mother's condition had worsened, she had been admitted to hospital and would I accompany her there the next day. The daughter had been a concert pianist. She lived in a most beautiful home, with not one piece of furniture out of place, and she was apparently care-free. But sadly, she appeared never to have loved her mother's Saviour. She was a charming woman, but with no sense of her need of Christ. When I had put the receiver down at the end of the conversation, I realised tomorrow could well be a traumatic occasion. I fell upon my knees and prayed that God would equip me to help this dear lady in her great hour of need, and her daughter also. A verse of Scripture, seemingly from nowhere, (have since become aware it was from heaven) broke in upon my mind - "When I am weak, then am I strong". [19] Without getting off my knees, I reached out for my Bible upon my desk. It literally opened at the very same words.

The next day the daughter and I drove to the nursing home, situated in the midst of beautiful pine trees in Surrey. I shall never forget the moment we walked into her private room. We were confronted by a corpse-like figure. For a moment we thought we had come too late and I heard the daughter gasp behind me. To be frank, my own flesh froze for a moment. Then, recovering myself, I stood beside the bed and spoke to the motionless form. I addressed her by name and then said "I have found your hymn:-

'Let me come closer to Thee, Lord Jesus,
Oh, closer day by day'"

YOUNG HEAVEN

Then something constrained me to utter the words God had given me the day before in my study, "When I am weak, then am I strong". - The immediate impact had to be seen to be believed! Within ten minutes, she was sitting up and asking for her Bible. Her daughter was amazed and so too was the matron, who passed through the room on her rounds, with her following retinue. She looked and looked again in sheer incredulity and then, speechless, moved on. It is difficult to convey the tremendous sense of God's presence we felt that afternoon. We knew heaven on earth, and what an old Scottish divine, Samuel Rutherford, called "Young heaven and young glory". I remember looking outside and seeing the pine trees pointing to the sky, and thinking they are pointing to where she is going - heaven. I would have liked more than anything else at that moment to have stayed beside the old lady and gone up to heaven with her. As the afternoon drew on, I realised it was time to leave, and it dawned upon me that I would never see her again in this life. My parting words to her came crowding into my mouth, "You know the Lord Jesus Christ is with you". I shall never forget her heavenly radiance and her sparkling blue eyes as she made her response, "Yes, and it's wonderful". I quietly walked away, so her daughter could have the remaining moments with her, but I could not but hear her mother's last words to her, "Learn to love the Lord Jesus Christ". I heard the daughter's step behind me and, seeming involuntarily, she said, "Mr. Bassett, how can we not believe?" Unmistakably "Precious in the sight of the Lord is the death of His saints".

SWEET ATHEIST

That evening I was due to take a mid-week Bible study in my church. I just had to scrap it and recount God's powerful dealings with that woman. The effect, though unknown to me at the time, was immediate. A young girl, who all of us took to be a sweet Christian, walked home, realising she was not a believer. My parting question to the whole meeting haunted her, "Would you be ready to die tonight?" She knew she was not, but within a few weeks she broke the news that shook my little village church, "I have been converted", and we discovered to our amazement that rather than a sweet Christian, she had been a sweet atheist.

The next Saturday evening I asked her to tell her story to the young people. It is helpful to recount that for two years I had seen no breakthrough for God. The young people were totally indifferent to Him. I introduced Judith, and after she had spoken I walked back to my house, which was situated in the grounds of the chapel. After a little while, I could see a young woman walking towards the house. She was a maid in the village, who attended the meeting. She was a sweet soul, but could hardly read or write. "I don't know God like her" she blurted out. "But do you want to?" I challenged her back. She confessed she did, but felt she would not be able to form a prayer. I told her that if she began to pray God would help her, and so He did. The dear lady's going to heaven, not only brought her daughter to believe, saw an atheist transformed into a radiant Christian, a humble maid into a quiet believer, who soon began to read and write, but about a hundred young people in a few years came to know the way to heaven and received Christ as their personal Saviour. To me was granted another view of a heavenly person, and "Heaven came down and glory filled my soul".

From that day, I have carried a card in my diary with the prayer of that godly woman. I have also given it to many people in different parts of the world.

"Let me come closer to Thee, Lord Jesus,
Oh, closer day by day".

Scripture References

1. Hebrews 10: 38
2. Hebrews 12: 1
3. Romans 4: 12
4. Genesis 5: 21-22
5. Jude 14
6. Romans 5: 12
7. Amos 3: 3
8. Hebrews 11: 6
9. Deut. 33: 25
10. Genesis 5: 24
11. Hebrews 11: 5
12. Luke 3: 22
13. Hebrews 11: 8-10
14. Hebrews 11: 13-16
15. Hebrews 13: 14-15
16. Eccl. 3: 1-8
17. Hebrews 44: 13-16
18. Psalm 116: 15
19. 2 Cor. 12: 10

5

Heaven - Time of Departure

In a letter I read a few minutes ago, the writer penned these words, "The time of my departure is at hand". [1] If the man in the street were to hear those words over the media, he might well imagine that some celebrity was about to embark on a world tour. But it was not so!

The writer was simply saying in his own inimitable way that he was soon going to die. Yes, he was daring to speak of the unmentionable - in a word, death. And his name? Paul, alias Saul of Tarsus.

A former Jewish religious and moral genius. He was a man who, before he became a Christian, had been guilty of having many believers in the Lord Jesus Christ, both men and women, put to death.

When the first Christian was martyred, young Saul had to be there witnessing every stone as it struck Stephen. Though it is not recorded that he threw one missile, it does state of the witnessing that they "laid down their clothes at a young man's feet whose name was Saul", [2] who was "consenting unto his death".[2] I will let Paul, formerly Saul, speak with his own fearful word - "I verily thought with myself that I ought to do many things contrary to the name of Jesus of Nazareth. Which thing I also did in Jerusalem; and many of the saints did I shut up in prison, having received authority from the chief priests: and when they were put to death, I gave my voice against them". [3]

Now all this I suggest is necessary reading for us to note how we may come to grips with the whole question of death; not as an end in itself, but as a preparation for heaven.

MURDERER OF CHRISTIANS

In fact for Saul of Tarsus, the murderer of Christians, on his way to harass other believers, it was heaven which stopped him in his tracks, for "As he journeyed, he came near Damascus; and suddenly there shined round about him a light from heaven, and he fell to the earth". [4] The bare facts of his conversion are that he is brought to realise he has been fighting, not merely against the Christians, but against Christ Himself, being literally blinded for three days by the brightness of the heavenly light. In a darkened room on Straight Street, Damascus, his life is changed for ever. He repents of his sin, believes in Christ, is baptised and "straightway he preached Christ".[5] Then during a lonely period of heart searching in the wilderness of Arabia, God reveals Himself to him.

From then on until the time of his departure, his life's motto is "For me to live is Christ and to die is gain". [6] Again he says "In nothing I shall be ashamed, but that with all boldness, as always, so now also, Christ shall be magnified in my body, whether it be by life or by death". [6] Is this mere bravado? No, these are the words of a man who thought his Christian life was to be seeking to win the world back to God at fearful peril to himself. So that he could literally say he had been "in deaths oft". What was his secret recipe for facing death constantly and longing for heaven? As Paul now said at the end of his life, in confinement in prison in Rome, "To die is gain". Does that sound ridiculous? Yes, it does without Christ. But Paul knew that to die was not a loss, for it was to gain Christ and heaven. In his own words, it was "having a desire to depart and to be with Christ, which is far better". [6]

Paul was like an extended piece of elastic, pulled in both directions at once. He desired to be pulled towards heaven, even through the doorway of death. But he realised that it was better for the sake of those for whom he cared, that he remained on earth to finish his ministry. The pull of earth, for the time being, kept his feet on the deck of this world and the pull of heaven must wait.

As we have seen, he had faced death many times for Christ's sake. He did not fear to die, because he knew that to be "absent from the body",[7] was to be immediately "present with the Lord".[7] He was able to look into the yawning grave and face the sting of death fearlessly and with faith, because he knew death was not only a gain and not a loss, but a victory not a defeat. He unashamedly wrote about this matter, literally challenging death - "O

death where is thy sting? O grave where is thy victory? The sting of death is sin; and the strength of sin is the law. But thanks be to God which giveth us the victory through our Lord Jesus Christ". [8] Paul saw that Christ on the cross and by his rising the third day from the tomb, had defeated death. He had borne the "sting" or the punishment and pain for our sins, which He knew the law of God demanded. Indeed:-
"Up from the grave He arose,
With a mighty triumph o'er His foes".

DOORWAY INTO HEAVEN

He has made the grave but a doorway into heaven and everlasting life. The grave for a believer is a door and death is stingless sleep, due to the victory of Christ. Paul also saw that due to Christ's resurrection from the dead, everything was changed. A glorious, endless future in heaven awaited every true believer in His atoning death for sin and His rising again. This is the linchpin of Christianity. We can do no better than quote Paul's immortal words to the Corinthian Church:-

"And if Christ be not raised, your faith is vain; ye are yet in your sins. Then they also which are fallen asleep in Christ are perished. If in this life only we have hope in Christ, we are of all men most miserable. But now is Christ risen from the dead and become the first-fruits of them that slept. For since by man came death, by man also came the resurrection from the dead. For as in Adam all die, even so in Christ shall all be made alive. But every man in his own order; Christ the first-fruits; afterward they that are Christ's at his coming". [9]

Later in this amazing chapter Paul writes about the resurrection. He shows that God will give us a body that will be perfectly conditioned to live in the pure environment of heaven above. "In a moment in the twinkling of an eye" [10] when God's trumpet call to heaven will come, we will be dressed in a new body, to meet the King of Kings. Our natural body will be exchanged for a spiritual one, to live in God's holy world. We will be recognisable people and our new body will be sinless, incapable of pain, decay, sorrow or death, because we are to live in God's home, which is described in three words, "**Incorruptible, undefiled,** and that **fadeth not away**". [11] These three words mean there is one of the "many mansions" (rooms) promised by the Lord Jesus for those who believe in Him, a house whose foundations will never crumble, in a city which has no pollution problems, with a garden whose flowers have a bloom that never fades, and the petals never fall. That is heaven in three words - again I say, "Incorruptible, undefiled, and that fadeth not away, reserved in heaven for you". [11]

DRESSED IN GOD'S CLOTHES

Finally, Paul glories in the anticipation of being dressed in God's own clothes; the immortality of God Himself - "So when this corruptible shall have put on incorruption, and this mortal shall have put on incorruption, and this mortal shall have put on immortality, then shall be brought to pass the saying that is written, Death is swallowed up in victory". [10]

Yet we must say again that in heaven we shall have bodies, and there will be an identity in our heavenly body, which we had in our earthly. There is something that will never be lost. In answer to the question, asked down through the centuries - "But some man will say, How are the dead raised up and with what body do they come?" [12] God clearly feels himself insulted by such a question, by the rebuke behind the immediate answer, "Thou fool, that which thou sowest is not quickened except it die". [12]

Paul then makes us look into a farmer's hand and see the grain in his palm, that he is about to sow in the ground. Can there be a greater difference between that corn of wheat and the harvest that will come from it after it has rotted in the earth? So God plainly says, "And that which thou sowest **thou sowest not the** body that shall be, but bare grain, it may chance of wheat, or some other grain. But God giveth it a body as it hath pleased him, and to every seed his own body". [12] Elsewhere the Lord Jesus Christ said of His own forthcoming death, "Verily, verily I say unto you, except a corn of wheat fall into the ground and die, it abideth alone; but if it die, it bringeth forth much fruit". [13]

GREATEST WORLD HARVEST

So the death of Christ is to be compared with the sowing of the seed, and His resurrection to the great world harvest. Heaven will be that harvest time. How wonderful to know that "as we have borne the image of the earthy, we shall also bear the image of the heavenly". We shall have a body like Christ's in heaven, but only if we know the Lord Jesus Who said, "I am the resurrection and the life: he that believeth in me, though he were dead, yet shall he live: And whosoever liveth and believeth in me shall never die. Believest thou this?". ¹⁴ The tragedy of these words is that merely uttered by a clergyman walking before a coffin, with mourners in a procession, if the one whose funeral it was not a believer, they are alas spoken too late. Yet there is enough in these words to carry any man in the world to heaven, whatever he has done, or whatever he has been. They tell us the greatest news in the world - that death for the believer is not the end, but the beginning. What wonderful words of hope and assurance these are concerning those we have known who have died believing in Jesus Christ's death for their sins, seeing it should, rightfully, have been their death, and His punishment theirs also. There is no greater comfort in this world concerning our loved ones, than to know "He that believeth in me, though he were dead, yet shall he live". Ultimately, this assurance is not given by a church, nor a minister, by by the One who has risen again, conquering death. It comes from the very lips of One who describes Himself "I am the resurrection and the life". Let us realise that the resurrection is not, in the end, merely the greatest historic event of hope, nor a truth tucked away in thin India paper in our Bibles but a Person. The most powerful Person, who has laid in a grave for three days, then neatly folded His death clothes and discarded them as unneeded for ever. The One who very early one morning walked away from death in new clothes, in which He lived for six weeks on this earth, before returning to heaven. We have as much certainty of seeing true Christians in heaven as we have of seeing Christ.

NEVER DIE ETERNALLY

Then Christ, secondly, has a word for us who are still living on this globe and are believing in Christ as our risen Lord. It is, "And whosoever liveth and believeth in me shall never die". That means shall never die eternally. Oh! yes, of course, our bodies will die, but we will not. We shall live on eternally. We have no more chance of dying than God has. What a word from God this is, "I give unto them eternal life, and they shall never perish". ¹⁵ The day we believe in Christ, God places His own godly, spiritual, everlasting life in us and we begin to live for ever. That can be a known reality built on the past victory of Christ over the one who had the power of death. No death in human history has been so documented as that of

Jesus Christ and one of those recorded facts into which faith can be bedded today is "That through death He (Jesus Christ) might destroy him that had the power of death, that is the devil". [16]

In that final moment on the cross, Christ our Saviour stripped away from Satan the power of death. And Christ, the risen Lord, gives us in its place the gift of everlasting life. Wherein then, lies the death problem, which should be but the point of departure for heaven? In a word, it is fear - the fear of death. Yet, if we did but believe it, those last moments of Christ on the cross were directed to that fearful enemy of man - fear. Indeed it is not readily appreciated that Christ in His lifetime took a body that was subject to death. The living God took unto Himself for thirty-three years a dying humanity. In that body, He groaned, sighed, wept and bled His way towards death. When He was in that dark Garden of Gethsemane, His flesh did no more want to die than ours. It cried out, "Father, if Thou be willing, remove this cup from Me; nevertheless not My will but Thine be done". [17]

GRACE TO DIE

On this whole subject, we can recall the tender and sympathetic advice the great Victorian preacher - Charles Haddon Spurgeon - gave a fearful woman. For health reasons he had gone to Mentone on the French Riviera. One day, as the residents of the hotel where he was staying were called to lunch, something in him made him not follow the others to the meal table, but instead go and sit outside the hotel. In a few moments he must have realised that Providence had placed him on that seat. For along came a woman, who must have recognised the famous preacher, and asked if she might share her problem with him. He beckoned her to sit down beside him and then asked her to tell him what it was. "The fear of death" she burst out. "Is it the fear of death or the fear of dying?" his profound God-given wisdom responded. "The fear of dying" she sighed. Spurgeon sympathetically agreed with her. He then suggested to her one or two ways in which she might die. One was if a fiery chariot like the one which took Elijah up to heaven landed on the French street corner and awaited her departure. Fearfully the timid woman, followed by Spurgeon himself, declined such a vehicle to transport them to heaven. "I'll tell you what I believe. You will go to bed one night and wake up in heaven" was the gist of what the great man prophesied, and it came true. Clearly Spurgeon kept up with the woman, for she died in the literal manner both of them hoped. He also made a remarkable statement during that conversation outside the Hotel Riviera - "When we come to die, God will give us enough grace to die".

Once when I was preaching, I recounted this story. Sometime later, a member of my church who had a very dear husband and four beautiful children, when she had just seen them off to work and school respectively, began to feel violently ill. She was certain she was dying. She was in the house alone, and there was no way to reach her husband, as he was still travelling on the train to London. She fell on the bed and then, in addition to her physical distress, there came sudden spiritual distress that, believing herself to be dying, she could not commit her four children into the hands of God. In her now moment by moment increasing anguish, she rebuked her unbelief, as she was a most godly young woman. Then like a flash, all of her foreboding was lifted in a moment. She realised she was not dying after all. God had brought back Spurgeon's words quoted in my sermon, "When you come to die, God will give you enough grace to die". She not only did not die, but is very much alive today. Maybe such a story is reassuring, for who is the believer who does not have doubts about this eternal destiny or preparedness to die.

SHALL NEVER SEE DEATH

Another fear of man awaiting his departure from this world, is to face the actual moment of death. What will it be like? Will it be darkness and chill, a black river playing at our feet and then slowly rising to our necks until it covers us and carries us away. Oh! there are, I believe, forgotten words of Christ which can comfort us at that moment more than any other words in the world. They are these - Christ says "Verily, verily, I say unto you, if a man keep my sayings, he shall never see death". [18] Do you ask, whatever does that mean? It means that the sole condition for knowing God's comfort in death, is our obeying Him in life. Have we simply obeyed His gospel out of sheer love for the beauty of His person, the wonder of His words, the glory of His death, and the endlessness of His life imparted to us? In a word, Christ said "He that hath My commandments and keepeth them, he it is that loveth Me; and he that loveth Me shall be loved of My Father and I will love him and will manifest Myself to him". [19] His promise to a person who obeys His sayings is "He shall never see death". There is a nuance = a hidden meaning - which conveys the thought that a dying believer's focus is not on the sight of death, but upon Christ, the conqueror of death. He will close our eyes to all else but Himself.

In my first Church was a middle-aged woman, who earlier in life had wandered away from Christ and married a Muslim. During a long illness from cancer, her faith became radiant. When she came to die, she looked around the room, with a remarkable expression on her face, then laid back and died. Her still Muslim husband who was present said to me "I am sure she saw her Lord".

Another, a much older man, a quiet self-effacing Christian, not given to anything like visions or revelations, had been in a coma for several hours, his wife remaining by his bedside throughout this time. Suddenly, he opened his eyes and clearly focussed them on his Lord, for all he said was one word - "Jesus!" and he was gone to heaven. Clearly neither of these saw death any more than the first Christian martyr, Stephen did. As he stood before his persecutors "All that sat in the Council looking steadfastly on him, saw his face as it had been the face of an angel". [20] Later when his very words convicted them of their sin, "They were cut to the heart and they gnashed on him with their teeth. But he being full of the Holy Ghost, looked up steadfastly into heaven, and saw the glory of God and Jesus standing on the right hand of God". [21] Not only did he literally see into heaven, not with the eyes of faith, but with his own mortal eyes, but he confessed it with his own tongue, "And said, Behold I see the heavens opened and the Son of Man standing on the right hand of God". [21]

HEAVEN OPENED

Stephen was clearly given the ability miraculously to see with his own eyes beyond this world. With God-given sight, he saw the Lord Jesus, amazingly not sitting, but standing. For Christ, since His return to heaven, has sat in triumph at God's right hand. He was the first priest in the world ever to sit in the presence of God the Father, because He offered the final blood sacrifice for our sins. It is vividly portrayed in these words - "When he had by himself purged our sins, sat down at the right hand of the Majesty on high". [22] What appears to have happened is that, as Stephen was standing up for his Lord on earth, and about to be stoned to death for his faith in Christ, the Lord stood up and drew back the curtain of heaven to look upon him. No doubt the angels who desired to look into these things, and the witnesses also, were there beside Him. There first appeared the reflection of the heavenly angels in the face of Stephen and as they pelted him with stones, he prayed "calling upon God", [23] the God whom he could see, standing now with opened arms to receive him. Now his prayers could be heard, "Lord Jesus receive my spirit". [23] And the sight of Christ standing in heaven made Stephen's blood-stained, yet worshipping form, to kneel down upon the earth. He never saw death, nor even those who put him to death. He saw heaven opened, Christ standing on the right hand of His Father, and the glory of God. Then his last words on earth must be addressed to God, "Lord lay not this sin to their charge". [23] The sight of Christ made him like the Lord Jesus - he prayed like Him in His death, for He had prayed from the cross, "Father, forgive them for they know not what they do". [24] It was as if Stephen were now oblivious of his foes, his agony, blind to everything and everyone save the Spirit of his Jesus and his heaven that he saw with his eyes though still on earth. He fell to the ground but beautifully he "fell asleep", [23] not like a marred martyr in death, but more like a child peacefully asleep in its mother's arms. Truly heaven begins here.

TELL MY PEOPLE NOW I LIVE

Another fear facing man is that death will be the end of everything. But we have seen from the words of Christ, that death for the Christian, is a beginning and not an ending. They "shall never die,"[14] is His great assurance to believers. Many years ago on a Saturday afternoon, I turned on my old radio set. I was amazed to hear the tramp of marching feet, and the music to which they were marching was "Jesus, lover of my soul". Without realising it, I was listening to the funeral service of the Dutch Queen Wilhemina. I was equally astonished to hear the soldiers were not slow marching. Then, unbelievably, I heard that all the royal families of Europe and the guests were commanded not to wear black, but white. Not only were no slow marches heard in the streets of Holland that day, but when the Queen's earthly remains were lowered into the ground, surrounded by royalties dressed more for a wedding than for a funeral, they sang a simple child-like Christian chorus learned and loved by Wilhemina as a young girl in a youth camp many years before, "there is a sunshine in my soul today".

She certainly did not "see death", but she left a message for her people and surely for us, "Tell my people, now I live". No, death for the true Christian is not an ending, but a beginning.

Scripture References

1. 2 Timothy 4: 6
2. Acts 7: 58 and 8: 1
3. Acts 26: 9-10
4. Acts 9: 3-4
5. Acts 9: 20
6. Phil. 1: 20-23
7. 2 Cor. 5: 8
8. 1 Cor 15: 55-57
9. 1 Cor 15: 17-23
10. 1 Cor 15: 52-54
11. 1 Peter 1: 4
12. 1 Cor 15: 35-38
13. John 12: 24
14. John 11: 25-26
15. John 10: 28
16. Hebrews 2: 14
17. Luke 22: 42
18. John 8: 51
19. John 14: 21
20. Acts 6: 15
21. Acts 7: 54-56
22. Hebrews 1: 3
23. Acts 7: 59-60
24. Luke 23: 34
25. John 11: 26

6

Preparing for Departure

Down through the centuries, perhaps heaven has become nearer to men when they have been near to the end of life's journey. In their last days, some have had such a sight of heaven, that they could not talk of anything else.

If one were to draw up a list of geniuses of all time, one would not dare to leave out Augustine, who was born in the fourth century. This great man was brought to realise that mankind was created by God and that he was restless till he found his rest in Him. He had a long search for this rest and was saved from a decadent life, mainly through the unceasing prayers of Monica, his mother. I want Augustine himself to recount for us parts of a conversation he had with his mother about the things of heaven, not long before her death.

"But the day was approaching when she (his mother) was to depart out of this life, though we knew it not. It happened that she and I were standing by a certain window, looking upon the garden of the house ... There we did confer 'forgetting those things which are behind, we reached out to those things that are before'. We enquired between ourselves ... what should be that eternal life of the saints in heaven, which 'the eye hath not seen, nor ear heard, nor hath it entered into the heart of man!' When our discourse reached such a point, the greatest delight of flesh and blood seemed unworthy to be remembered, or even compared with the sweetness of that life eternal. We made a kind of progress, not only to the vault of heaven itself, but higher yet, until we touched upon that region ... where Thou feedest Israel for all eternity with the food of truth ...

We two did stretch ourselves up ... to lay hold a little upon the eternal wisdom, that abides upon all things ... Would this be what is meant by 'Enter thou into the joy of thy Lord?' But when shall this be? Shall it be when we all rise? ... Thou knoweth oh! Lord, that when we said such things, this world with all the delights grew contemptible, even as we spoke of it. Then said my mother 'My son, for as much as concerns me, there is nothing now in this life wherein I take delight. What have I yet to do here? ... Behold God has given me that for which I desired to stay in this life (the conversion of her son Augustine.) For now I see thee to be His servant. What then do I here any longer?'

Of his mother's sickness and death. 'Lay this body where you will' she said. She had prepared a grave close by the body of her husband. She desired ... to her other happiness might be added this, that the same earth might give burial to their two bodies. But I found by that very speech she used to me when she said 'What do I here any longer?', she discovered no desire of dying in her own country. Afterwards talking with friends she said, 'Nothing is far off from God, neither is there any cause to fear that at the day of judgment, He will not know well enough from what place He is to raise me again.'"*

Now some may say, "I'm just an ordinary person, I'm no genius, can ordinary people have a great sight of God and heaven at the time of death?"

One of the humblest and plainest people I ever met, used to travel about six miles by train every Sunday, come sunshine or snow, to worship with our village congregation. I shall never forget her coming to my house once, and pushing into my hand an old plaque, with these words, "Sir, when you look upon this plaque, remember how near you brought me to heaven". With that she was gone. Now whether she had some premonition concerning her death, I do not know, but one evening shortly after this, my wife and I had asked a couple into dinner. I was talking to the husband, who was a self-taught man, who apparently had moments of inspiration that could save the country a few million pounds. We had been talking about faith in God helping us in all situations with which we may be confronted in life. I had just said, "You know, we must live very close to God, because we never know what is going to happen the next moment." Those words were like a cue in a play, for at that second the telephone rang. It was a call from a hospital several miles away to say this humble woman who had given me the plaque was dying, and asking for me.

GONE TO BE WITH GOD

It was about 11.00 o'clock when I eventually reached her bedside. They were giving her oxygen, and clearly she had not much longer to live in this life.

"You're racing me to glory then" I said, when there was an opportunity to speak. I often wonder what the two young nurses attending her thought, as we had heavenly conversation together. "Sir" she responded, "You have left heaven in my heart." Then she paused and her facial expression changed. "'Don't see the minister, see the Lord' that's what you once told me in a sermon" she recalled, "That's better" I agreed. Beside the bed that night sat her old auntie, a very hard and mean woman, who, when her niece came to stay, would put her in a shed at the bottom of the garden. She clearly thought the dying woman was so inferior. "Fifty pounds for your chapel extension" broke in again my friend in the bed. I don't remember what I said, for I did not believe she had that amount in the world. Then the sweetness of heaven came and filled the dying woman's life, and she could not stop talking about God and the Bible. Then, exhausted, she fell asleep, her breathing rapid and labouring. At 4.00 o'clock in the morning she woke up. "You still here sir" she uttered in amazement to see me sitting there. "It won't be long now" she assured me, as if she were waiting for a bus to come, rather than death. Heaven came down, and as I quoted comforting Scriptures to her, faintly and increasingly more feebly, she finished off the verses. Finally I said to her, "Ask". She barely replied "And it shall be given you. "Seek", "and ye shall find" she managed to say. "Knock" "and it shall be opened unto you "[1] she gasped and went through the door of heaven. It was 7.30 precisely on the Saturday morning. I drew back the hospital curtains surrounding her bed and stepped back into this world. "Has she gone?" came the gruff question, breaking the silence. She seemed to be like a vulture waiting for its prey to expire. "Gone", I replied "Gone to be with God". It was like the closing moments of a film. The silence was only broken by the sound of my footsteps. Yes, ordinary people go to heaven, sometimes with heaven already in their hearts. She knocked and God opened His door and let her in. He opened the front door, and not the servants' quarters. Certainly not the shed, for there are no sheds in heaven.

LIGHT OF ETERNITY

But you may say, "I don't believe in God, let alone in heaven". But, I remind you, you do believe in death. One afternoon, the blunt but searching question "What about death" was put to me by a hard and unbelieving nursing sister, dying of cancer. It was one of those prepared lives that opened like a flower to hear that Christ had already died her rightful death for her sins and taken her place. I assured her that there was nothing to fear once she trusted in Christ as her Saviour. I believe that very day she began to prepare to meet God by asking Him into her life. You may say, there is nothing very remarkable about that. Wait a moment! She soon had to go into hospital for the last time. I was due to go on holiday, but felt constrained to pay her a last visit. I knew we would not meet again in this life, and these were my last words to her. "When we meet in heaven, you will say 'Paul, you didn't tell me half'". When I returned from holiday, she had already left for heaven. I went to visit her husband, who had formerly shown no interest at all in the things of God. "You know Mr. Bassett" he said with a very serious face, "My wife lived the last week of her life in the light of eternity". Truly, the hardest heart can be softened, and, even here, the half about heaven has never been told.

I promised in the preface that this book would help people to prepare for heaven. The hardest thing, perhaps, a minister has to do is to try and help dying young people or children. Of course, this is a harrowing experience for the parents. My wife often reminds me that God plucks some of His flowers when they are very young. I finish about a teenager, the other an eight year old girl. The first account will be brief, and the second I feel to recount as it took place.

REACHING THE UNCONSCIOUS

One Sunday morning a total stranger approached me after morning service. She told me this pathetic story. Briefly it was, that her beautiful daughter had fallen into a coma at the age of about twelve. Now she was eighteen, she could not show any bodily or facial response to her mother's voice or touch. One vital point I recall was that her daughter as a little girl trusted Christ as her personal Saviour. Her dilemma was, could God still reach her daughter? All though lunch, I turned her question over and over again, but I could not think of any answer. Turning out of my drive on my way supposedly to comfort the mother, a thought broke in upon me which to this day I believe came from heaven. It was simply this; God is not dependent upon the body as we are. He can deal directly with the soul. Normally our body receives and transmits messages for all to see, but this is not essential.

I never got to see the girl, for a day or so earlier, she had left behind her now useless body and gone to heaven to await a new one. At the moment of death, her mother told me she felt to pick up her daughter, but still there was no visible response. Then as the girl breathed her last breath, her face became radiant and remained so for several minutes. The nurses could not believe it, and least of all could her reluctant father, who had to be coerced into the room to see his daughter's face. He told me at the funeral, "You have preached to me of God this afternoon, and my daughter's face preached to me of God at the moment of her death!" Without a doubt, heaven came down and glory filled her soul.

Finally, I feel to insert the record of the death of a very young child. I want to so do, because some parents I have met, faced with a similar tragedy, have gained great comfort and even faith through Nicola's story.

ONLY A MONTH TO LIVE

I first visited Nicola's home just before Christmas, 1975. I had not met her before. I only learned of her - and of the fact that she had leukaemia - after a member of our church had called at her home and discovered her condition.

That member's visit was itself an answer to the prayers of a group of Christians in a near-by town, who knew of her need, and were praying for me by name to go to her house. One member of that group had offered to contact me, but finally felt, they should simply pray and leave the matter with God. A friend of Nicola's mother had even driven up and down past my house, but had felt restrained from coming in to share the burden, lest it lead to intruding into Nicola's home. Christian ministers are not always welcome.

Nicola was only eight and her parents knew how hopeless medically her condition was. She had been surrounded by their deepest love and attention, but they admitted that they had never prayed, nor even read Bible stories to her.

Heart-ache. I had long, long talks into the night with the parents, sharing their heart-ache, their questions, their fears. I sought to assure them. "If this is the only life" I said, "then all this agony would be meaningless; but if it brings both of you and Nicola also really to know God, it will be worth it in the end".

Why suffering? I felt I must not attempt to side-step the question of "Why suffering?" So I talked to them of the beginning of the world and showed that suffering and death entered the world the day that man first sinned. [2] Yet I quickly added that God was neither cruel, nor vindictive, as though choosing to punish people with suffering. Rather, suffering and death had now become a part of life. Even Job, the holiest man of his day, suffered: even God's holy Son had suffered.

Perhaps out of respect and gratitude for my visits to the home, the three of them came to the church carol service. My theme that evening was that the Lord Jesus Christ came into the world "to seek and to save that which is lost". I noticed that Nicola was restless through the sermon.

I still continued to visit Nicola and her parents, until there came the terrible "day of truth": they were told that Nicola only had about a month to live. Only eight years old - and the last chapter of Nicola's life was about to begin. But that was the very time God chose to begin to write the first chapter of her new life. It was then that God allowed me really to speak to her for the first time about God and prepare her for heaven.

INJECTIONS?

"Do you like injections?" I began, knowing that she had had more than her fair share. I told her of some Royal Air Force medical orderlies I knew who had for fun once cruelly tried to turn an officer into a pin-cushion - to see how tough he really was! I also told of the medical orderly who was so different, no one ever really felt his injections - or forgot his life.

One day he volunteered for a special flight, which later crashed in Germany. They found his dead body unmarred, but covered with little cards carrying verses of Scripture. They had fallen out of a small folder, on which were written these words "Wherewithal shall a young man cleanse his way?... Thy word have I hid in my heart that I might not sin against Thee!"

I remember saying to Nicola, "What a way to go to heaven - hiding Jesus in your heart!" There was such a wonderful expression on her young face. "You see, Nicola" I added, "it's rather like the way the old Jews thought of heaven - as going upstairs to God". I then told her how this young airman had become a Christian. A young Christian had seen some airmen standing on the corner outside his church just before the evening service. When he invited them to come to the service, they all went away except this young man. He went in and that evening believed on the Lord Jesus as his personal Saviour from sin. Within six months, he was in heaven with his Saviour. I could see from Nicola's face that God had begun to write the first chapter of her new life.

Nicola's father had promised me that he would come to church the next Sunday evening. As he was changing and getting ready, Nicola asked him where he was going. He told her and she begged him to take her along. He answered her that he dare not, in case she caught a cold; the doctor had said that if she got the least infection at this time, it would end her life - and the 'flu epidemic was at its height. So her father left for church alone.

MOTHER'S TURN

Now it was mother's turn for "the treatment". Nicola said that she would go outside and catch a cold if she didn't let her go to church. Grabbing her coat, and her lively sheep-dog Tom for company, she put her threat into action in the cold night air. "Why ever has Nicola got this urge to go to church?" thought her mother. She had never seen her in such a tantrum, and Nicola had been told it was for her own good to stay away from crowds of people.

Realising that church was very important to the child, her mother quickly threw on her own coat, put Nicola into the car and arrived at church during the singing of the first hymn. She asked for a place to sit where they could conveniently leave after ten minutes. They were directed to "the ten minute seats" near a convenient side door, and a grimacing mother and a beaming daughter made their way past the astonished father, who joined them at the rear.

RADIANT FACE

Both mother and father watched Nicola constantly, but she was so enraptured and her face so radiant, that there was no question of leaving after a few minutes, in spite of any 'flu germs. I had been told that her father would be present, so I was expecting him. Then half-way through the sermon, I saw her mother and thought to myself, they must have a baby-sitter. Only near to the end of the sermon, did I see Nicola as well.

That afternoon I had been very bothered over the advisability of preaching on the ten lepers. I had imagined how her father might think: God healed all the ten lepers - couldn't He heal my little one? But God made me preach that sermon that night and, like the one leper, one little girl turned back and thanked God. At the end of the sermon, she turned to her parents and said: "I am going to thank him for that lovely sermon". I shall never forget the radiant face as she came down the aisle towards me, her face shining, and said just "Thank you for that lovely sermon". Really she was saying "Thank you" to the Lord Jesus. I told her: "Now you can go home with Jesus". That night back at home, she said, "He was speaking to me", and added that she would be going to church every Sunday in future, morning and evening.

On the Tuesday following I called and left her a little card with the words of a hymn she came to love, "Let me come closer to Thee, Lord Jesus, closer day by day". I told her how she could make that her prayer.

I was in contact through the week following, but on the Friday night I felt I must go again. She ran into the hall and kissed me and said with her Bible open: "I've found the book of Daniel, but I can't find Daniel in the lion's den!" I sat her on the arm of the chair, and with her parents present, told her simply that life was sometimes like a lions' den, but that the Lord Jesus would still come to us in the den of lions. The four of us had an unforgettable time together. It was all young heaven and young glory! She said, "I wish it was Sunday tomorrow, and what are you going to preach on? Oh! I wish I could go to church every day!" I thought to myself that her prayer would soon be answered.

The next Sunday night she bounced into church and on the Wednesday into heaven. After listening to the sermon that Sunday night, she went home and listened to the whole service of the previous Sunday on cassette. Before getting into bed, she flung herself on her knees and prayed. On the Monday morning she played with her little friend Sarah, and in the afternoon with my little boy. But she was getting tired. At bed-time she became ill and spent a sleepless night.

ALWAYS SUNNY THERE

Early next morning she implored her mother to telephone and ask me to come to her. When I arrived she said, "You know, it's always sunny in heaven every day, there is no night there". Then later, "I am looking forward to going to heaven, but you will be there first" (because I was older!) I told her, "It is a case of when God calls us. When He calls us, we go". She didn't ask me what I meant, but I believe she knew. I reminded her that in a sermon I had said that there would be a crown which would only fit her head. She answered, "And the robe!"

Later that afternoon, her parents took her into hospital. The next dawn was the last on this earth for Nicola; exactly one month to the day as the doctor had predicted. During the first part of the morning a laboratory technician visited the ward. She told me she was a Christian and that when she had come to pray for Nicola that morning, she had had the strong feeling that God already had her in His keeping. That was an amazing comfort to Nicola's parents. We sang hymns to her. I read, "In my Father's house, there are many mansions" and then reassured her of the crown and the robe waiting for her.

TOP OF THE STAIRS

I told her "You are nearly at the top of the stairs". Believing she still had an hour or two in this world, I felt I should read Psalm 23. I read "The Lord is my Shepherd, I shall not want", and began to think - what am I gong to say to her when I have finished this Psalm? I felt I was going to dry up. I continued reading to the last verse, "And **you** will dwell in the house of the Lord for ever". She turned her little face on the pillow. There was such an expression of peace, for she had reached "the top of the stairs". I called after her, "Asleep in Jesus ... Absent from the body, present with the Lord - see you in the morning".

We knelt down and gave thanks for her life.

A little child has led me to a deeper knowledge of the Lord, and others, - in her own family and beyond - have since come to know her Lord and Saviour.

"You know" Nicola once said, "the power of the cross conquers all evil". Have you proved that through coming to know Christ?

So from the earliest era of the Church, from Augustine's mother down to the present century, Christians have found that heaven begins here, with the hope put by God in their hearts, and they look forward to being with Christ, which is far better than anything this earth can offer.

How wonderful to contemplate that each time a Christian dies, though we witness a departure, heaven witnesses an arrival.

Scripture References

1. Luke 11: 9
2. Romans 5: 12
* Excerpt from The Confessions of Augustine, book 9

7

*T*he *Ascent*

"I did think I did see all heaven before me, and the great God Himself". So wrote Handel when he composed the music to the 'Messiah' in twenty two days, during which time he scarcely ate or slept. It has often been as with Handel, when men have been rebuffed and written off by the world, that they have equally turned from faith in man to faith in God.

TOUR UP TO HEAVEN

It needs to be said, as we approach the end of the twentieth century, that heaven is still open. God's door is ajar and He is most definitely open to seekers and to those who will stay to view His spectacular home, with all its angelic and seraphic contents.

Two years after Handel wrote that most unforgettable sacred music that truly seemed to come from heaven itself, Edward Payson slipped unnoticed into the world and was born in New Hampshire, in America in 1783, later to become a minister of the Gospel in Portland. I have never forgotten the words I am about to quote. They only confirm powerfully that whilst down here on earth, we are meant to live in "The Holiest" (which is another beautiful description of heaven.) Payson describes his most memorable domestic scene as follows - "At the beginning of the evening, before the candles are brought in, if I am at home, which is not very often the case, we all sit down and take a little tour up to heaven and see what they are doing there. We try to figure to ourselves how they feel, and how we shall feel and what we shall do; and often when we try to imagine how they feel, our feelings become more heavenly; and sometimes God is pleased to open to us a door in heaven".

When Solomon had finished building the largest place of worship in the world, God gave him a divine directive what to do if He chose to shut up heaven. Solomon was literally sitting or standing there one night when God appeared to him. In fact, he often had visits from God in the night, no doubt when Solomon was less busy. We are told "And the Lord appeared to Solomon by night and said unto him, I have heard thy prayer and have chosen this place to myself for a house of sacrifice. If I shut up heaven that there be no rain ... God then set out a key for man to use to open the door of heaven from the outside - "If my people, which are called by my name, shall humble themselves and pray and seek my face, and turn from their wicked ways; then I will hear from heaven and forgive their sin and heal their land." [1]

God lays down a principle for civilisation in these words. A sin sick society is in that state because heaven is shut up to earth and no blessing falls upon proud, prayerless and wicked people. That is not too strong a description of any land or nation in the world, which has ceased to pray to heaven for its deepest needs to be met. Man is too proud, generally speaking, to humble himself and pray. Therefore heaven is shut up and man remains unforgiven in God's sight. "History teaches us that history teaches us nothing" was the Hegelian maxim that sadly lives on in today's world. If we trace the wanderings of God's people spiritually, we would see that Israel's forty years of failure can be summarised as follows, "Because they believed not in God and trusted not in His salvation, though He had commanded the clouds from above and opened the doors of heaven, and had rained down manna upon them to eat and had given them of the corn of heaven". [2] Heaven for them was like a huge market daily opened by God. Amazingly we are told "Man did eat angel's food: He sent them meat to the full" [2] We cannot say that every drought and famine is a judgment of God upon man, for that would be a wicked inaccuracy, yet, at the same time, the spiritual condition of man largely determines whether heaven's door is open or shut, and accordingly, whether our needs are met or not. Heaven has not merely many doors but many windows also. Yet sometimes it is sadly true that, due to man's ignorance, all are shut. God says to such people, "Ye have not because ye ask not. Ye ask and receive not, because ye ask amiss." [3]

STEALING GOD'S WORLD

Every man in ancient Biblical times set aside the first tenth of his crops or possessions for God, and from heaven he was blessed accordingly. But, as time went on, man thought it was better if he held the purse strings! And for centuries heaven's windows were shut up. Because man sought to "steal" God's world from Him and all its contents, which were really the gifts of God, through the open door of His home above.

It would be good if in the Kremlin, the White House and in Whitehall, they asked the question, why is heaven more often shut up than open? When will it be opening time again? God gives a brief panoramic sweep of a people knowing little of the dew of heaven, and writes concerning them, "Even from the days of your fathers, ye are gone away from my ordinances and have not kept them. Return unto me and I will return unto you saith the Lord of Hosts. But ye said, wherein shall we return? Will a man rob God? Yet you have robbed me. But ye said, wherein have we robbed thee? In tithes and offerings". [4]

Worse, He says that such people are cursed with a curse. This could be the greatest reason for the weak and sickly church generally speaking throughout the world today and, as we have noted, the sin-sick society which its fails to impress. We must return to God and cease robbing Him of His money, gifts, talents and time, and He has only loaned us for seventy years or a few more. Let these words ring in our conscience - "Ye are cursed with a curse, for ye have robbed me, even this whole nation." [4]

The need of that hour, is the need of this, church-wide, nation-wide and world-wide. God says, "Bring ye all the tithes into the storehouse, that there may be meat in mine house, and prove me now herewith saith the Lord of hosts, if I will not open the windows of heaven and pour you out a blessing, that there shall not be room enough to receive it". [4] Does not God say still today, "If my people ..."

It is not too naive an understanding of the history of the Church and of the nations, to say that the natural and spiritual blessings are governed by God and our failure to return to Him and prove what blessings would fall from heaven.

But there is another sense in which heaven is open for men, women, young people and children through the way opened by Christ's death, to visit God's home, when through the rending of the veil of the temple, a way of access was provided. Yet we should never forget how desperate ancient men were for God to open the heavens and visit this needy world with His presence. Is there a more passionate prayer for God to do this than "Oh! that thou wouldest rend the heavens, that thou wouldest come down, that the mountains might flow at thy presence". [5]

A LADDER TO HEAVEN

But it is an entirely new dimension to know what it is to ascend into heaven. Our first step up the ladder must be prayerfulness like Christ, "Jesus also being baptised and praying, the heaven was opened". [6] Another rung upon the ladder must be a guileless spirit, typical again of Christ. He detected such a spirit in a certain man sitting in secret under a tree, thinking no doubt of heaven and desirous of getting there. Then, "Jesus saw Nathaniel coming to Him and saith of him, behold an Israelite in whom is no guile". Then He said, "When thou wast under the fig tree I saw thee" [7] To such a seeker of God and His abode, the Lord promises, "Hereafter, thou shalt see greater things than these, verily ye shall see heaven open and the angels of God ascending and descending upon the Son of Man". [7]

If the Queen of Sheba literally swooned when she visited King Solomon and particularly when she saw "his ascent by which he went up into the house of the Lord, there was no more spirit in her" [8], it pales into insignificance compared with King David, who encouraged the men of his day to become ascenders to heaven. He describes further rungs upon the ladder by a flow of questions, the answers to which show spiritual movement upward. His first question to present day heaven seekers is "Who shall ascend into the hill of the Lord and who shall stand in His holy place?" [9] He is seeking men like they sought for the first men to climb Everest or more recently, to go up into space, and even to the moon and soon beyond. The world vitally needs heaven seekers. The answer to David's question is descriptive of the next rung, and the character of the person who is to put his life upon the ladder. The answer comes back from God via David's lips, "He that hath clean hands and a pure heart" [9]. The cleaner the hands, the purer the heart, the higher we ascend to the hill of the Lord, the peak of Paradise, the highest altitude. We shall then be in His holy place, more certainly and more permanently than our astronauts stood on the moon. A further two steps to be overcome are vanity and deceit, which aid our descent from God, rather than our ascent to Him. We must therefore be sure " He... who hath not lifted up his soul unto vanity, nor sworn deceitfully. He shall receive the blessing of the Lord". [9] Those daring David-like climbers to heaven were known in their day as a group apart, described as "This is the generation of them that seek him, that seek Thy face ..." [9]

SPIRITUAL MOVEMENT

There is what one must call spiritual movement in the Christian life. Of course there was such when we came to discover that from being way out, "Now in Christ Jesus, ye who sometimes were far off are made nigh by the blood of Christ". [10] My friend, don't stop there. The hymn is right when it says, "Nearer, still nearer, close to thy heart".

But how and when shall this come about?

Often when we look at ourselves, we have to admit, perhaps reluctantly, "But as for me, my feet were almost gone, my steps had well-nigh slipped. For I was envious at the foolish, when I saw the prosperity of the wicked". [11] But at last we saw their true standing in God's sight and were forced to confess, "Until I went into the sanctuary of God, then understood I their end". [12] From then on, God becomes our most desirable person and heaven, clearly, our most desirable place. So, as we step higher on another rung of the ladder, which is that of desire, we can cry out "Whom have I in heaven but thee, and there is none upon earth that I desire beside thee". [13] All we want to do then is to declare "But it is good for me to draw near to God" [13] There then remains but one higher step - to enter heaven itself. Yet it seems that even in New Testament times, the majority held back from the boldness needed to seek for God and heaven. One of the writers shows us the way, "Having therefore brethren boldness to enter into the holiest by the blood of Jesus" [14] - Christ's blood has opened a new route to heaven - "by a new and living way, which he has consecrated for us through the veil, that is to say his flesh. And having a high priest (i.e. Christ) over the house of God; let us draw near, with a true heart in full assurance of faith, having our hearts sprinkled from an evil conscience and our bodies washed with pure water" [14] Look at the spiritual movement - ascend, stand, draw near, "enter into the holiest". That is the highest habitual experience of the Christian. It is a foretaste of heaven itself. "Let us **draw near** with a true heart in full assurance of faith ..."

FLY LIKE AN EAGLE

As the Holy Spirit flew in the form of a dove through the rent in heaven's curtains to Christ (at His baptism), it is equally possible as we wait upon God to "fly" like an eagle to heaven. Such words are so poetic that if we do not really think about them, we may lose the sheer wonder and encouragement of their meaning, but we can literally "mount up with wings as eagles" [15] and fly to heaven. It has been said that the eagle is the only bird that can look the sun directly in the face. Let us rather look the Son of Righteousness in the face. We shall be like those patient but persistent people who stand near the gates of Buckingham Palace hoping for a glimpse of the Queen. God promises "blessed is the man that heareth me, watching daily at the posts of my gates, watching at the posts of my doors". [16] Here it seems that we have been brought within the very gates of glory and only the open door is between us and a new vision of the King of Kings in His Royal Palace above. They may be disappointed outside Buckingham Palace, but we shall not be, for the heaven "watcher" is assured "For whoso findeth Me findeth life, and shall obtain favour of the Lord". [16]

How vital is it to understand that God never intended that man should be merely earth-bound. For decades modern man has interpreted this to mean that he should learn to fly like a bird and even to say "fly me to the moon". But God has been concerned for man, not to break the sound barrier, but the heaven barrier. He has not been so interested for man to travel to the moon and back, I suggest, but rather that he would go to heaven and back; a wonderful reality that men and women of God have known down through the centuries.

THE THIRD HEAVEN

Such a man was Paul the Apostle, who when describing his heavenly experience, hides with characteristic humility behind the introductory paragraph to his story in these words - "I knew a man in Christ above fourteen years ago (whether in the body I cannot tell; or whether out of the body, I cannot tell: God knoweth) such as one caught up to the third heaven." [17] He wanted to go to heaven anonymously! Paul had felt for fourteen years to remain silent and not go into print - let alone eternal print! But as God took him up to the third heaven, it was God who made him tell us about it. He was "caught up" by God. For it is He who must take us up to heaven, even whilst on earth. This is nothing new, for God's word to men living in Old Testament times was, "Get thee up to the high mountain". [18] Such was the experience of Moses, who, in the midst of lightnings and thunderings, received God's tablets of law. Then in New Testament times we recall how Jesus led up three men, Peter, James and John, into the mount and was transfigured before them. God's personal invitation to man still reads today - "Come up higher".

Now this was what Paul knew when he was caught up to the third heaven, which he also calls Paradise. Paradise was the place to which Christ ascended from Calvary where He was crucified. For when the dying, now believing criminal hanging on the cross at His side, sought for Jesus' reassurance as he cried to Him, "Lord, remember me when Thou comest into Thy kingdom" [19], Christ answered him, "Today shalt thou be with Me in Paradise" [19]

UP INTO PARADISE

Does this mean that like Christ, Paul's soul went up into Paradise? It appears to be the case, for Paul no longer worried at that moment about his body. For he says more than once "whether in the body or out of the body I cannot tell: God knoweth". What an honour for one's soul to rise and dwell in the place of Paradise, the home of the soul of one's crucified Saviour. But even the inspired Apostle dared not mention the words which were spoken to him by God in that holy place. They were words spoken for his ears only and not for any others.

It is true to say that heaven will not be so strange and unknown a place as some people think. For every experience of Christ in heaven will already been felt in embryo on earth. The only difference will be that our sinfulness which blinded us to the manifestation of that glory of Christ on earth and chilled our hearts at times to be like stone towards Him, will all be gone. "Then shall I know even as I am known" [20] You see Christ will be no different when we meet Him in heaven, than what He is this day on earth. It is no use singing "All may change, but Jesus never, glory to His name" if we do not believe it. And, above all else "Jesus Christ the same, yesterday, and today and for ever" [21] means that the Christ of yesterday's earth and today's earth, will be the same as forever's heaven.

TESTIMONY OF THE THORN

Yet Paul did not stay caught up in heaven. He knew what it was to go there and to come back. And for the remainder of his life on earth he bore the marks of that visit to Paradise, in that he humbly admits, "Lest I should be exalted above measure through the abundance of the revelations, there was given to me a thorn in the flesh". [22] It did not keep him from taking the heaven he had experienced back to men on earth, even more because the weakness in his flesh kept him dependent on God and yet made him touched with a feeling for those like him who had a painful testimony - the testimony of the thorn. He said later "Ye know how through infirmity of the flesh, I preached the gospel unto you at the first. And my temptation which was in my flesh ye despised not, nor rejected; but received me as an angel of God, even as Christ Jesus". [23] He goes on to say "Ye would have plucked out your own eyes and have given them to me". [23] That was Paul's thorn, the price paid for going to heaven and back, in some degree - a loss of sight.

POWER WITH GOD

Hundreds of years before this a man called Jacob, a deadly deceiver by nature, was left alone, and in his loneliness he wrestled with God, continuing even with the breaking of a new day. Truly sometimes "The kingdom of heaven suffereth violence". [24] So even in the midst of his combat with the angelic wrestler, Jacob vowed "I will not let thee go except thou bless me". [25] The price was a new name for Jacob - Israel - a prince, a prince of Paradise, of "power with God and with men and has prevailed". [25] Yet in the morning, Jacob's thigh was out of joint and the light of day broke upon his limping form.

Let us never forget that the One who first opened heaven, did so with bleeding hands and a pierced side; the punishment of men's sins upon Him - the punishment which even He could scarcely bear. Then Christ Himself went into heaven, and the Porter saw the price of opening Paradise in the perpetual scars of the Saviour. But mercifully Christ did not close the door behind Him; He left it open for us.

Since then heaven has been sought for and often even found by more than a few. Hundreds of years ago, in his day, Isaac Watts looked towards heaven, having read the 84th Psalm. He paraphrased it, but beyond that, allowed the hunger of his soul to remain as a lasting legacy for today's heaven seekers.

"My soul how lively is the place
To which thy God resorts,
'Tis heaven to see his smiling face,
Though in his earthly courts.

There the great monarch of the skies,
His saving power displays;
And light breaks in upon our eyes,
With kind and quickening rays.

With his rich gifts the heavenly dove,
Descends and fills the place,
Where Christ reveals his wondrous love,
And sheds abroad his grace.

There mighty God thy words declare
The secrets of thy will;
And still we seek thy mercy there,
And sing thy praises still.

My heart and flesh cry out for thee,
While far from thy abode:
When shall I tread thy courts and see
My Saviour and my God?

The sparrow builds herself a nest;
And suffers no remove,
Oh! make me like the sparrows blest,
To dwell but where I love.

To sit one day beneath thine eye,
And hear thy gracious voice,
Exceeds a whole eternity,
Employed in carnal joys.

Lord at thy threshold would I wait
While Jesus is within
Rather than fill a throne of state,
Or live in tents of sin.

Could I command the spacious land,
And the more boundless sea,
For one blest hour at thy right hand,
I'd give them both away."

LIVING IN HEAVEN

One of the greatest men who ever lived was a man called Jonathan Edwards. He lived in Northampton, in New England, America in the 18th century. He was, possibly, the most eminent pure philosopher of his day, and also a minister, who stood as motionless as the flame of the candle burning in his hand, as he preached. His words carried heaven to the hearts of his hearers, whilst revivals of religion flowed from God through his life and lips. But his wife had gone a step higher than he. She had been to heaven, from whence those revivals had come. About that, her sane and saintly husband had no doubt at all. Thank God, like Pepys, many men and women were diarists, or kept a journal in those far off days, and, thankfully, Mrs Edwards records her heavenly days and nights. As the modern mystic Tozer found before his death in 1963, the greatest blessings are often "Born after Midnight".

These are some extracts from her journal:-

"Mr. Buell then read a melting hymn of Dr. Watts, concerning the loveliness of Christ, the enjoyments and employments of heaven, and the Christian's earnest desire of heavenly things; the truth and reality of the things mentioned in the hymn made so strong an impression on my mind, and my soul was drawn so powerfully towards Christ and heaven, that I leaped unconsciously from my chair. I seemed to be drawn upwards, soul and body, from the earth towards heaven; and it seemed to me I must naturally and necessarily ascend thither. At length my strength failed me and I sank down, when they took me up and laid me on the bed, where I lay for a considerable time, faint with joy, while contemplating the glories of the heavenly world."

ALMOST LEFT THE BODY

"I seemed to myself to perceive a glow of divine love come down from the heart of Christ in heaven, into my heart in a constant stream, like a stream or pencil of sweet light. At the same time, my heart and soul all flowed out in love to Christ: so that there seemed to be a constant flowing and reflowing of heavenly and divine love from Christ's heart to mine. I seemed to myself to float or swim in these bright, sweet beams of the love of Christ, like the motes swimming in the beams of the sun, or the streams of the light which come in at the window. My soul remained in a kind of heavenly elysium. So far as I am capable of making a comparison, I think what I felt during the continuance of the whole time, was worth more than all the outward comfort and pleasure, which I had enjoyed in my whole life put together. That sun has not set upon my soul all this night. I have dwelt on high in the heavenly mansions; the light of divine love has surrounded me; my soul has been lost in God and has almost left the body." *

In Volume 3 of the works of John Flavel, he tells of a man, a minister, who had such an experience of God that he said something to the effect that he learned more in that one moment than in fifty years of reading books about God.

Of that minister, he says:-

"Being alone in a journey and willing to make the best improvement ... of that solitude, he set himself to a close examination of the state of his soul ... then of the life to come, living in heaven ... and of all those things which are now pure objects of faith and hope. After a while, his thoughts began to come closer to those great and astonishing things than was usual: and ... his affections began to rise with liveliness and vigour.

He therefore lifted up his heart to God that He would so order it ... that he might meet with no interruption or accident in that journey; which was granted to him. For, he neither met, overtook or was overtaken by any. His thoughts began to rise higher and higher like the waters in Ezekiel's vision, till at last they became an overflowing flood. Such were the ravishing tastes of heavenly joys ... that he utterly lost a sense of this world and for some hours knew no more ... than if he had been in a deep sleep upon his bed. At last, he began to perceive himself very faint and almost choked with blood, which running from his nose, had coloured his clothes and his horse ... He found himself almost spent under the pressure of joy ... insupportable; At last perceiving a spring ... he alighted to cleanse his face and hands, which were drenched in blood, tears and sweat.

By that spring he sat down ... earnestly desiring that if it were the pleasure of God, it might be his parting place from this world. Death he said had the most amiable face that he ever beheld, except that of Jesus Christ Who made it so.

He said he could not remember ... that he had one thought of his dear wife, or children or any earthly concerns. But having drank of the stream, his spirits revived, the blood stanched, he mounted his horse again; and on he went in the same spirit, till he had finished a journey of nearly thirty miles ... greatly admiring how he had come ... that his horse, without his direction had brought him thither, and that he fell not all that day (in spite of) several trances. **

FORETASTE OF HEAVEN

The innkeeper came to him astonished, "O Sir" he said, "What is the matter with you? You like like a dead man". "Friend" replied he, "I was never better in all my life".

A supper was sent to him, which he could not touch ... All the night passed without a wink of sleep, though never had he a sweeter night's rest ... The joy of the Lord overflowed him, and he seemed to be an inhabitant of the other world. The next morning, he was early on horseback again ... but within a few hours he was sensible of the ebbing of the time ... though there was a heavenly serenity upon his spirit ... yet the transports of joy were over. He many years afterwards professed he understood more of the light of heaven by that day, than by all the books he had ever read or discourses he ever had entertained about it. This was indeed an extraordinary foretaste of heaven ... but it came in the ordinary way of faith and meditation. **

Coming right up to the present, in a little book "In His Time", which was sent to friends of the missionaries who were killed in the Manoram (Thailand) Hospital tragedy on the January 14, 1978, when 12 people died, there was a little poem, which had earlier been quoted by one of the surgeons who was killed.

It read:-

"Just think
Of stepping on shore and finding it heaven,
Of taking hold of a hand and finding it God's hand,
Of breathing new air and finding it celestial air,
Of feeling invigorated and finding it immortality,
Of passing from storm and tempest, and finding it calm,
Of waking up and finding it home."

That poem, of course, describes the ultimate, but we are concerned with those who have been to heaven and back, living in this world.

EARLY POP FESTIVAL

In case you think it is only the famous who are given that honour, I would say that heaven can come to those who are not seeking, let alone deserving it. I knew a young minister about thirteen years ago, who took sixteen young people to a remote Suffolk village to seek to win that place for God. He found that, humanly speaking, they had not only chosen the wrong time, but the wrong place. Six miles down the road, they were about to welcome over 100,000 young people to one of the early pop festivals. One of the men who had invited them suggested they worked at the pop festival rather than in the village. The leader felt otherwise. God had sent them to that village. On the last but one night of the mission, when the neighbouring youth would soon be around in its black leather and hell's angels gear on powerful motor bikes riding through those twisting, sleepy Suffolk lanes, God dealt with that minister so deeply that his heart was broken with such a sight of himself and his sin. Every word of God wounded him and he was kept in a flood of tears for hours. He had only gone to his car just for a few minutes to glance at a message, and then go and speak to the quiet, respectable village people. But God opened the heavens and revealed the depths of sin in his heart. His face and shirt were sodden with godly tears of sorrow, and he not only thought he would never preach again, but would never get out of that car again! At last he went into the village chapel, ashamed at what must have been the sight of himself. The place was packed with youths in black leather! God told him to sit down and not to speak until He told him. When he did rise, he read the fearful chapter of Ezekiel 33, warning the young people that if they ignored the command to turn to God, their blood would be upon their own heads. He did not really preach, but simply read. Then he knew he had to kneel down in the midst of those tough young people and pray for them. For the next four hours, the workers spoke to them. They never bothered to go to the pop festival! Later that night when he had arrived at the place where he was staying, he had such a sense of the sweetness of heaven, that he could not leave his car till the break of day. It seemed the saddest moment of his life that early morning, to realise he had come back to earth, even though he had the dearest wife and his son had just been born.

Later the devil sought to impress upon him that it had been all emotion, and he agreed with him! That night might have been the end of it, had he not put his hand upon a little book of C.H. Spurgeon's called "Till He Come", and the first message was entitled "Mysterious visits". It described what that young minister had known with perfect exactness. Spurgeon writes of God giving men visitations which are firstly "sharply searching" and then "sweetly solacing". This convinced the one who had gone through those experiences that they were truly of God.

The famous Dr. Samuel Johnson said of John Wesley, the great Methodist preacher, "I could talk with him all day and night too. I found in him a habitual gaiety of heart. He is the most perfect specimen of moral happiness I ever saw. In Wesley's speech and temper, I discovered more to teach me what a heaven on earth is like, than all I have elsewhere seen or heard or read, except in the sacred volume".

We may well say, a tribute indeed to John Wesley.

I feel I must close this chapter by briefly describing the most holy, Christlike and heavenly man I ever met.

He was an elderly, radiant Jamaican, attending the church where we worshipped in London. He was sitting alone, with the most remarkable face you ever set eyes on. There was something there that had not come through natural birth. On his lapel he unashamedly wore a badge with "Jesus Saves". He sat unnoticed by the two hundred or more round him drinking their after service coffee. Their loss was our gain. Next Sunday we welcomed him for the day, and on subsequent occasions for longer stays when he visited this country to attend Home Office courses. It is easy to say that he brought the joy of Christ and the happiness of heaven under our roof. Yet it was never an austere happiness, but attractive and Christ-exalting.

MYSTERIOUS FIGURE

One night before going to bed, we asked him to tell us how he came to know God. As I recall, he was about eighteen years of age, when his best friend suddenly died.

A day or two afterwards when he was lying down one afternoon, not asleep, yet not fully awake, a mysterious figure came and stood at the foot of his bed and with a frightening countenance pointed at him with a rod, simply saying in an ominous voice, "You will be the next". He was awake in a moment, and from then onwards, his life was so haunted by the fear of his imminent death. Worse than that, he was aware he was not ready to meet God.

Then, one afternoon, he felt to pray to God to come to his aid. He then laid down on his bed again and in that identical condition one sometimes experiences when one is half awake, the same mysterious figure came again and stood at the foot of his bed.

This time there were two differences. The first, the countenance was a shining one and at the end of the rod pointed at him, there was a star. Then his heavenly visitor quietly and invitingly asked him to "Follow Me". For the next thirty-six hours, this young man was taken up into another world and tasted Paradise. He was quite oblivious during that time that several of his friends and relatives came and looked upon his motionless form lying on the bed. They were for trying to bring him back to consciousness, as they feared he had fallen into some form of sickness or coma. But from nowhere a little West Indian woman slipped into the room and said with a quiet and authoritative discernment, "Leave him alone, God is dealing with him", and so He was. Our Jamaican friend told us how he was led through fields and pastures more beautiful than he had ever seen on his own island, unusual birds flew about him, and he heard singing, with which no choir on earth could compare. At last he said, the man who was leading him stopped by a riverside and told him to kneel down. Then he pronounced some seraphic benediction upon him, with such words as these, as I recall, "Be baptised, be sanctified, be filled with the Spirit". Our friend stopped speaking and an awe filled our lounge. The silence was broken at last by his simple conclusion, "How could I ever be the same again?" And to that testimony, all who have been to heaven and back, would heartily, yet humbly adhere.

Scripture References

1. 2 Chron. 7: 12-14
2. Psalm 78: 22-25
3. James 4: 2-3
4. Malachi 2: 7-10
5. Isaiah 64: 1
6 Like 3: 21
7. John 1: 47-51
8. 2 Chron 9: 4
9. Psalm 24: 3-6
10. Ephesians 2: 13
11. Psalm 73: 2-3
12. Psalm 73: 17
13. Psalm 73: 25-28
14. Hebrews 10: 19-22
15. Isaiah 40: 30-31
16. Proverbs 8: 34-35
17. 2 Corinth 12: 2
18. Isaiah 40: 9
19. Luke 23: 42-43
20. 1 Corinth 13: 12
21. Hebrews 13: 8
22. 2 Corinth 12: 7
23. Galatians 4: 13-15
24. Matthew 11: 12
25. Genesis 32: 26-28

* Extract from the works of Jonathan Edwards Vol. 1 ch. 11 page LXIV-LXV
** Taken from the work of John Flavel, Volume 3 pp 57-8
Banner of Truth Trust

8

What Heaven is Not

A great painter will usually introduce shade and darkness into his picture, to make the light stand out with the greatest possible effectiveness. Likewise the wonder of Christ's triumphant death and resurrection stands out with very great impressiveness against the backcloth of His poverty, loneliness, persecutions, temptations, denials, betrayal and finally - and fearfully, His own followers forsaking Him.

So, when God would paint the glory which is heaven, He follows the same line of approach. He begins by showing what heaven is **not**, so that by comparison we may come to appreciate what heaven **is**. And I believe that God in His perfect wisdom, has seen fit to show us His wonders mainly in the last book of the Bible; no doubt to keep us in anticipation, but also to see that the whole of the life of man is meant to be preparation for that which is to come. As we have seen, heaven begins **here**; it is a foretaste of what we shall be there. We will merely exchange in the twinkling of an eye, present anticipation for future realisation.

FELL AS DEAD

The great apostle John, the apostle of love, as he has been affectionately called, was exiled for his belief in Christ, to the isle of Patmos. Aged, alone and cut off from friends and homeland, he found that when he was banished from the familiar world, heaven was opened to him. There came a day when he was given such a wonderful and mysterious vision of the risen Lord, that he, who had rested his head on the breast of Christ in the

Upper Room, he who had seen Him transfigured on the mount, came to see more of Christ by the Spirit, invisibly, than he ever saw in the three years living with Him when He was on earth.

He simply writes these amazing words, "When I saw him, I fell at his feet as dead". [1] What a paradox - a man almost dying at the sight of the living God. Like Ezekiel and Daniel before him, John was literally prostrate before God. Then a door was opened in heaven (from the inside - God's side) - and from then on he gives us God's own description of His many mansions in the sky - in a word - heaven.

NO MORE CURSE

The simple two letter word "no" is the most perfect to describe heaven. God gives us first a negative approach. In the wonderful twenty-second chapter of Revelation, God's last word, it is seen to be a place where "there is no more curse".[2] That must be our starting point, because the earth, since the fall of the first man into sin, and the subsequent fall of the whole human race, is under the curse of God. Therefore, whereas Heaven is a place of blessing, so negatively, it is described here as having "no more curse".

Christ came to earth to remove the curse, which sin had brought upon all mankind and replace it with His blessing, for Christ bore the curse or the punishment of the violated law of God in His own body on the tree. Vividly and graphically the Bible declares that "Christ has redeemed us from the curse of the law, being made a curse **for us**, for it is written 'Cursed is everyone that hangeth on a tree'. [3] Amazingly, the God who pronounced the curse of the law on all mankind, met the penalty of His own law. Christ in His life on earth kept the law man had broken, and in His death He bore the penalty. That is why He agreed to be born of a woman and placed Himself beneath the violated law of God. The fruit of the accused life of Christ is sweet to the taste of faith. "There is therefore now no condemnation to them that are in Christ Jesus". [4] Because Christ has been cursed instead of us, we are blessed because of Him. Yet, look around the city where you live. Walk its hospital wards and hear the effects of the curse in every cry of pain, see them in every disease, in every demented expression, in every death. Go to your crematoriums and your cemeteries. The roses in rows do not hide the hideous tomb-stones that speak of the curse for man, for a death man needed not to die. He lost Paradise and exchanged the blessing of living for the curse of dying. The world laughs at Adam and Eve, but they do not laugh at death, and it just will not go away. The voice of the curse is still with us, for man has never been willing to go back to the beginning and see where it came from. Just read the first book in the world, - the book of beginnings - in a word Genesis. "And unto Adam He (God) said Because thou hast hearkened unto the voice of thy wife and hast eaten of the tree of which I commanded thee not to eat of it; cursed is the ground for thy sake; in sorrow shalt thou eat of it all the days of thy life; thorns and thistles shall it bring forth to thee: and thou shalt eat the herb of the field; In the sweat of thy face shalt thou eat bread, till thou return unto the ground; for out of it wast thou taken: for dust thou art and unto dust shalt thou return". [5]

NO WEED-KILLERS THERE

Because in heaven there is no curse, never will sweat run down from the brow, because labour will be no more. No weed or thistle or thorn will ever rise from heaven's earth; no weed-killers there! The very last sigh will have fallen from human lips, simply because it is written, "And there shall be no more curse". The word "no" is often a bitter word on earth, but in heaven there will be none sweeter.

NO NIGHT THERE

As I write the day is drawing in and night is about to fall. I shall never forget reading a newspaper around midnight on Midsummer's day in Norway, but in heaven night will be no more. It will not be needed, for night is the God-given friend of rest for the worn-out mind and body and even nature needs to sleep. But in heaven, man would be like God who neither slumbers nor sleeps. Again, every cause of stress and strain will have been removed. Man will have a perfect mind and a perfect body, which will never need the night season for rest, nor will there be anything to weary him whatsoever. Here the night is endless when we are burdened in our souls. Who has not known this, "My sore ran in the night and ceased not; my soul refused to be comforted". [6] Soon dear reader, in Christ that will be no more.

Again, some of the worst sins are done under the cover of night and darkness. No wonder God's word would stir Christians to leave the night of sin and all its shady companions. No wonder God has to speak to us so firmly and so directly and say, "But ye brethren are not in darkness that that day should overtake you as a thief. Ye are the children of light and the children of the day. We are not of the night nor of darkness. Therefore, let us not sleep as do others, but let us watch and be sober. For they that sleep sleep in the night, and they that be drunken will be drunken in the night".[7]

At least three nights will have flown away for ever - literal night, the night of sin and the dark night of the soul. The last thread of care will have been shed, we will have slept our last sleep, sinned our last sin, and known gone for ever the dark night of the soul. We can do no more until that day of light than to hear God say, "Who is among you that feareth the Lord, that obeyeth the voice of His servant, that walketh in darkness and hath no light? Let him trust in the name of the Lord and stay upon his God".[8] "until the day break and the shadows flee away".[9] What a thought. "There shall be no night there".[9A] Roll on nightless heaven!

4) NO MORE SEA

In heaven, there will be "no more sea,"[9B] and therefore no more navy; only saved sailors. There will be no more world cruises to try to find paradise on earth, because we will have found it in heaven. The last nuclear submarine will have submerged for ever, because there will be no more war. No cargo vessel will travel the sea, because heaven will be stocked with everything man needs. Above all else, we will need the sea no more, because there will be no more journeys, for whatever purpose, whether uniting friends or separating loved ones. It is comforting that the so-called cruel sea is under God's control, as is the earth also. "And God called the dry land earth, and the gathering together of the waters called He seas".[10] God has placed boundaries upon the sea, showing who is really sovereign in that "He hath compassed the waters with bounds"[11] and commands the waters with devastating effect, "And said, hitherto shalt thou come, but no further, and here shall thy proud waves be stayed".[12]

5) NO MORE HUNGER

Then, heaven is a place where there will be no more hunger or thirst. It is put so beautifully that we need to read and re-read it, whilst we are in this barren desert, this dry, dry old world, this waste howling wilderness of a world. It says, "They shall hunger no more, neither thirst any more, neither shall the sun light on them nor any heat. For the Lamb which is in the midst of the throne shall feed them, and shall lead them unto the living fountains of waters". [13]

Heaven is the end of the famines. Yet right up to the end of time, Christ forecast famines with such words as these "For nation shall rise against nation, and kingdom against kingdom, and there shall be famines and pestilences and earthquakes in divers places". [14]

We have seen that in heaven we will have "a spiritual body", that is not corruptible, that is, it does not need the constant nourishment of natural food to strengthen it and restore the burnt up energy expended through the sheer effort of living.

Many of the early Christians suffered from physical hunger, because of the remoteness of the places they pioneered to bring God to a lost and isolated world. They "launched into the deep" like Livingstone. They went into the interior of the unevangelised lands, like the Misses French and Cable, two fearless women who crossed the Gobi desert for God, and knew deprivations that were indescribable. Of the ancient Church of God, Israel, it is recorded, "hungry and thirsty their soul fainted within them". [15] Our Lord was in the wilderness with the wild beasts for forty days and forty nights. This was no hunger strike to draw attention to Himself, but rather He was wrapped in mortal combat with Satan. Luke the historian recorded in his gospel these words, "Being forty days tempted of the devil. And in those days he did eat nothing. And when they were ended, he afterward hungered". [16]

Paul declared of himself and the other apostles, "We both hunger and thirst and are naked". [17] Yet incredibly, they did not moan or grumble, or even beg, let alone have an appeal week. I often wonder, will we in the Western world ever really know God again, wrapped in the materialistic strait-jacket of our plastic civilisation. We have turned luxuries into necessities and believed that economic security spells success, also the right recipe for a life of contentment on earth, whereas these men had a different education system in their world. They learned in hunger and in suffering, rather than in plenty and in ease, whilst modern man designs a world free from such things, in order to create an utopic paradise on earth. How many of us can say with the pioneer of Christianity, Paul, "I have learned in whatsoever state I am, therein to be content ... I am instructed ... to be hungry and to suffer need". [18] In the Bible, strangely, Christ is seen as the Man of hunger and of thirst. Those who have given away their last loaf and water in a chipped cup, have unknowingly fed Christ and quenched His parched lips. Every true Christian must heed the word to "deal thy bread to the hungry" [19] and face the bare boards of this text tucked away towards the end of the New Testament, "If thy brother or sister be naked and destitute of daily food, and one of you say unto them, Depart in peace, be ye warmed and filled, notwithstanding ye give them not those things which are needful to the body, what doth it profit. Even so, faith, if it hath not works, is dead, being alone". [20]

The feeders of Christ's hunger and the quenchers of Christ's thirst will not get to heaven for that reason alone, but because it will have issued out of faith in Him as the living bread and in Him as the living water. Christ says such righteous people will go away "into life eternal". [21]

Incredibly in heaven, the place of no literal hunger or thirst, we shall ever remember each time we look upon Christ, that we had the privilege of being allowed to **meet His hunger and thirst on earth.**

NO THIRST

But, beyond that, the non-hungering and non-thirsting in heaven refers also to the end of spiritual hunger and thirst.

Let us say categorically that the desire for God will never die, but dissatisfaction will. Christ will fill the hungry and thirsty souls finally and fully by feeding them Himself, for "The Lamb which is in the midst of the throne shall feed them ..." Even in this life, we have to wrestle with this spiritual paradox or apparent contradiction in that Jesus said unto them, "I am the bread of life, he that believeth on me ... shall never hunger".[22] A man, woman or young person bringing their emptiness, the fearful hunger of soul for Christ, to God, begin from that moment to feed upon Christ in the same way as they feed physically upon daily food. I believe it means we will never find anything else to feed us and satisfy us, once we have really fed upon Christ.

Jesus satisfies and we will cry out with the Welsh poet, William Williams, "Feed me till I want no more". The food of Christ turns our taste from everything else on the menu of man.

In heaven we shall perfectly know the happiness of heart and soul contentment. Did not Christ promise even on earth, "Blessed are they that hunger and thirst after righteousness for they shall be filled", [23] and again, "As the heart panteth after the water-brooks, so panteth my soul after thee O God. My soul thirsteth for the living God". [24] Don't give up this side of heaven. Cry this day to Him, and you will find heaven begin here. God promises to "Guide thee continually and satisfy thy soul in drought and make fat thy bones, and thou shalt be like a watered garden and like a spring of water whose waters fail not". [25]

Even here, "He satisfieth the longing soul", [26] and then in heaven we shall know this, "As for **me**, I will behold thy face in righteousness. **I shall be satisfied** when I awake with thy likeness". [27]

7) NO MORE PAIN

One of the greatest fruits of the agony Christ suffered for us on the cross is that there will be no more pain. Because the last book of the Bible tells us "Neither shall there be any more pain". [28] Because of all He bore for our sins on earth, we shall know no pain above. Christ indeed when He was born took a body subject to pain and infirmity, that is excepting sin. He totally identified Himself with us, not taking an angel's form, but a human body. "For verily, he took not on him the nature of angels, but he took on him the seed of Abraham". [29] He did so, "Forasmuch then as the children are partakers of flesh and blood, he also likewise took part of the same: that through death he might destroy him that had the power of death, that is the devil". [29]

Christ, therefore, directed His whole life to us in our pain and ultimately dying and rising again, to remove it for ever. For no man can conceive the agony He bore on the tree physically, as the nails were driven into His hands and feet, and all His bones were dislocated, when the cross was driven into the socket on the ground. He "himself took our infirmities (literally our weaknesses) and bare our sicknesses" [30] God made Him weak, that we might be made strong. It was as if He were made sick, that we might in heaven no more say, "I am sick". [31] No wonder when people called for Jesus to come, they would simply say, "He whom thou lovest is sick". [32] That was enough! He came at once to the bedside and, suffering friend, He still comes when we call.

But many suffer with mental pain and anguish in this life. The forsaken husband or wife, the unwanted child, the unloved discarded person, the wounded and the care burdened. These all need the prescription for mental suffering - to be brought from perplexity to peace. I hardly know of any more appropriate advice than this, "Be careful for nothing, but in everything by prayer and supplication with thanksgiving, let your requests be made known unto God". [33] When we pour out our hearts to our friends and neighbours, we so often hear the words, "Stop worrying; it will be all right in the end". Now on the surface these glib words seem the same advice as God's. Man's advice so often stops at "Don't worry", but God's does not. He goes on to say, "But in everything by prayer ..." In down to earth language, God is saying to you, "Stop worrying about anything, and start praying about everything!"

But is your mental pain still troubling you, and yet you haven't prayed? Are you holding back because you say, will God answer my prayer? Then just listen. The verse continues, "And the peace of God which passeth all understanding, shall keep your hearts and minds through Christ Jesus". [33] Prayer is the pathway that leads from perplexity to peace, but it is God's peace and not man's.

Before He left this world, Christ said, "My peace I give unto you, not as the world gives give I unto you. Let not your heart be troubled, neither let it be afraid". [34] Prayer is the heavenly prescription of the Great Physician of peace and it is God's own everlasting peace. Someone has said, "Peace is the reflected smile of God in the soul of the believer". Christ has done this, "having made peace through the blood of His cross". [35] When His blood touches our sins and our failings, it brings instant peace. When we take the excruciating pain of our unbearable burden of sorrow and tragedy to Him, we only then begin to experience, to discover that the peace of God is beyond our human comprehension.

Finally, here the picture is so beautiful and so comforting. Paul was a prisoner. As he wrote these words, and as he saw the Roman soldier guarding him, God whispered to him to take up his pen and write of the peace of God that would "keep" (stand sentry or guard) over hearts and minds through Christ Jesus. You, shut up in your prison of pain, whatever form it takes, realise there is one watching over you. The Prince of peace wants to come and turn your prison into a haven of peace and to help you anticipate the palace of painlessness in heaven, where there will be no more pain. Let the attractiveness of that prospect introduce you here below to the peace of God that indeed passes all understanding.

We do not know what led Katherine von Schlegel to write the words of the hymn, but their comfort is carried like heavenly cargo down through the avenue of the years to us today:-

"Be still my soul, the Lord is on thy side,
Bear patiently the cross of grief or pain.
Leave to thy God to order and provide,
In every change He faithful will remain.
Be still my soul, thy best, thy heavenly friend,
Through thorny ways leads to a joyful end.

Be still my soul, the hour is hastening on,
When we shall be for ever with the Lord,
When disappointment, fear and grief are gone
Sorrow forgot, loves purest joys restored.
Be still my soul, when change and tears are passed
All safe and blessed we shall meet at last."

NO MORE TEARS

In heaven there will be no more tears, for "God shall wipe away all tears from their eyes; and there shall be no more crying". [28] The pain of tearfulness here will make us appreciate the preciousness of tearlessness there. The Saviour had eyes that could shed tears. The briefest, most dramatic, most compassionate words in the world were possibly "Jesus wept". [36] If man had not chosen sin, he would never have learned to weep, whether for sin, or for sickness, for sorrow, for solitude, separation, or for suicide. Our tears are generally selfish, but Christ's were always selfless. They flowed from Him, but not for Himself. He wept by the grave of Lazarus, which even bystanders were forced to acknowledge showed "Behold how he loved him (Lazarus)". [36] Yet it was accompanied by a groan from Christ, as He witnessed at closest hand the ravages that the entry of sin and death had executed on a human life and body. No doubt His flesh anticipated His own death, His agony, His grave awaiting Him a few weeks hence. And He was to weep again over a city, because they knew not the time of His visit.

Who is the man or woman who does not weep and wonder can we ever be the man or woman we were for God, or would be for Him? How wonderful it is that our tears do not fall downward, but upward, overcoming the very law of divine gravity, and falling into the Saviour's heavenly tear bottle. Oh! to be able to know and say today "Thou tellest my wanderings, put Thou my tears into Thy bottle, are they not in Thy book?" [37] Soon, as you come up to Christ in heaven in prayer, you will really prove "Weeping may endure for a night, but joy cometh in the morning". [38] Perhaps you may be reading this book in the night of your tearfulness. But as you turn back to God, joy will come in the morning and, beyond that, is the morning of that TEARLESS HEAVEN. In that day Christ will take His heavenly handkerchief and wipe away all your tears, and it takes a very special person to do that. There will be nothing more to weep about, no sin, no lost sinners, no more separation, no more death of loved ones. Tears in this life are in the Saviour's safety valve of the soul. Tears are sometimes moist, voiceless prayers and sighs for the Comforter's presence. Those tears may fall, but they go up to heaven into the heart of God.

Until that tearless morn of heaven dawns, the world must have a generation of weeping preachers, which will produce a generation of weeping people. The world only knows how to weep for itself in pity; it has long since forgotten how to weep for its sins.

But there is need to "sound an alarm", [39] to turn the indifferent world back to God before it is too late, for it is coming to an end, and it is not ready to meet its master. "Therefore also now saith the Lord, turn ye even to Me with all your hearts and with fastings and with weeping and with mourning. And rend your hearts and not your garments and turn unto the Lord your God; for He is gracious and merciful, slow to anger and of great kindness, and repenteth him of the evil. Who knows if he will return and repent, and leave a blessing behind him: ... Blow the trumpet, sanctifying the congregation, assemble the elders, gather the children and those who suck the breasts ... let the priests, the ministers of the Lord weep between the porch and the altar, let them say, spare Thy people O Lord, and give not thy heritage to reproach, that the heathen should rule over them: wherefore should they say among the people where is their God? Then will the Lord be jealous for His land and pity His people". [39]

Before our church and our land be brought there, as it must be, to the coming judgment of God, may we see raised up the weeping preacher. Oh!

that we could say with Paul of his church that "he had been with them at all seasons, serving the Lord ... with many tears". [40] Today in our services we have many laughs, many jokes, but very few tears. Our pulpits and our pews are very dry.

We also need to be weeping writers. Paul again could say, "I wrote unto you with many tears". [41] There was for him no difference between the weeping words of his writing and his tearful speech over lost sinners, who mocked at Christ's death for them. Paul met their enmity with tears of compassion, and he could say, "Now I tell you even weeping that they are enemies of the cross of Christ". [42]

But dear reader, have you ever known tears for a lost Christ? Mary Magdalene could not live three days without Christ. Follow Mary's footsteps and see how even the sight of angels at Christ's tomb and their words which sought to comfort her, could not turn her aside from finding her lost Lord. No angel's words would do! She must hear again His "Mary" and she must respond "Great Master". [43] That alone stopped the copious flow of her tears. And that is why in heaven there will be no more tears. We will have found Him whom our souls love and will not let Him go.

NO MORE DEATH

Heaven for the believer will be the end of death - "There will be no more death". [28] As there was a beginning to it, there will also be an end. The day that man sinned at the first, death entered, "Wherefore as by one man sin entered into the world and death by sin, and so death passed upon all men, for all have sinned". [44] No wonder John Milton, the poet, sought to portray the shock to Adam, confronted by death the first time:-

"But have I now seen death, is this the way I must return to dust?
Oh sight of horror, foul and ugly to behold, horrible to think!
Horrible to feel!"

Death is a divine appointment, and there is a day when we shall keep it. There are, in fact, only two appointments we shall be sure to meet, one with death and the other with judgment. "It is appointed unto men once to die, and after this the judgment". [45] I can never think upon these words without recalling the first mission I ever embarked upon. I was visiting in a village street, and decided to make one more call before lunch. The day was cold, the man was not interested. I then asked him if he were ready to die, and face

God on the judgment day. He looked at me with scorn. "Death" he said, "is curtains". I opened my Bible and it literally opened at the very words I had quoted, and, even more fearfully, the index finger of my right hand was pointing at the same place. "What do you think of that?" I asked him. He stared in silent, speechless amazement. All the scorn and fight had gone out of him. His wife called him into lunch several times; she said the food was getting cold, then she said the draught would not be good for his back but he silently stared at God's word. At last, after what seemed an eternity, he turned without a word, his head bent, and a more solemnised man I never set eyes on. I doubt if he had any appetite for lunch, but I hope the day prepared him to keep his appointment with death.

Though every Christian will have to face judgment, on the other side of death, like every other person in the world, it will have no fear for him, because, "There is now no condemnation for them that are in Christ Jesus". [46] He knows also that the day is coming when death will be no more. For, "The wages of sin is death, but the gift of God is eternal life through Christ Jesus our Lord". [47] We have spent a previous chapter dealing with the way to face dying. Here we may see how Christ by His own death dealt finally with the last enemy itself. Our faith even now rests in the One "Who hath abolished death". [48] We have seen how Christ by the cross has taken the sting out of death. It cannot destroy us. He alone has faced and beaten it ("the last enemy"), [49] but for the Christian it is happiness as it hurries him into heaven, for "Blessed are the dead who die in the Lord". [50]

For the Christian, there is no fear of "the second death" [51] that is the eternal death of the unbeliever. It is terrible to contemplate that in hell they wish they could die, but they cannot. They are dying, but throughout eternity they never will. To reject everlasting life from God, is to choose eternal death in hell. Oh! there is nothing sweeter to know that "the second death" has no power over us. Surely there was no wiser proverb ever uttered than this one, "The way of life is above to the wise, that he may depart from hell beneath". [52]

NO CATHEDRAL

Does it surprise you to know that in heaven you will never worship in a church building; no cathedral, no church, no chapel will ever be built there. "And I saw no temple therein, for the Lord God Almighty and the

Lamb are the temple of it".[53] I can remember so well I also once thought of a church as a building, and not as God defines it, as the people of God, the redeemed of the Lord. "The church of God, which he hath purchased with is own blood".[54] What an eternal open air service that will be by day and by night. No computer will be able to count the great multitude there, "which no man could number of all nations, and kindreds and people, and tongues",[55] so it will be an international service, needing no minister to address the people, nor a choir master upon his rostrum. No sacred, so-called object will be allowed to detract from the spiritual worship of God Himself and the Lamb.

Do you remember how Christ broke through the feud between the Jews and the Samaritans as He led this outcast, unloved, immoral Samaritan woman to salvation? Not as an end in itself, but as a means to teach the pure, spiritual worship of God. It is to be dependent, not on place or posture, but totally upon God Himself and God alone. The Jew cannot hold on to his Jerusalem, nor the Samaritan to his Mount Gerizim. Wasn't Christ correcting the understanding of worship, and, incidentally, showing us heavenly in embryo. When "Jesus saith to her, Woman believe me the hour cometh, when ye shall neither worship in this mountain, nor yet in Jerusalem worship the Father ... but the hour cometh and now is when the true worshippers shall worship the Father in spirit and in truth, **for the Father seeketh** such to worship him. God is a spirit, and they that worship him must worship him in spirit and in truth".[56]

Oh! dear reader, we do not need the Gothic arches, the crosses and the crucifixes to lead us to worship God. Nor should we in reaction believe our simple chapels, swept and clean and often powerless, are the answer, nor those who feel they have found the New Testament pattern of worship in their house meetings. We are all wrong. God is the object and in His triune persons the forgotten glory of worship. The One who said on earth, "I will be to them a little sanctuary"[57], will be a great Sanctuary to us in heaven. There, there will be a simplicity, a spirituality, and a spontaneity in worship, of which we have never seen the like on earth.

One of the reasons why Christ did not close the door behind Him when He re-entered heaven and sat down in triumph at the right hand of the Father, was that we might see and hear the worship, which the sight of the praise-worthy person of the Lamb of God draws forth from every single worshipper and returns to the One who gave it, demands it and delights to inhabit the praises of His people. Just by faith, stop what you are doing, gaze through the door of heaven and behold, "four and twenty elders (no doubt representing the patriarchs of the Old Testament, and the apostles of the New, a complete and united Church) fall down and worship Him that liveth for ever and ever". [58] The singing would be unbelievably pure and perfect and God-directed - "And they sung a new song ... saying with a loud voice, Worthy is the Lamb that was slain, to receive power and riches and wisdom and strength and honour and blessing". [59]

One man of ancient times could say, "How amiable are Thy tabernacles O Lord of Hosts. My soul longeth, yet even fainteth for the courts of the Lord; my heart and my flesh crieth out for the living God ... blessed are they that dwell in Thy house: they will be still praising Thee". [60] Young and old worshippers throughout the centuries have said "Lord, I have loved the habitation of thy house, and the place wherein thy honour dwelleth". [61]

STANDING ON TIP-TOE

It has made man stand on tip-toe waiting in the expectation of it all. The sight of perfect worship in heaven should only make us men and women and young people of "one thing" - to see God and desire to seek Him now where we live and worship today. Oh! - that this may become the motto of our lives, "One thing have I desired of the Lord, that will I seek after, that I may dwell in the house of the Lord all the days of my life, to behold the beauty of the Lord, and to enquire in His temple". [62]

May the contemplation and the anticipation of the templeless heaven above, make us heaven-seekers and heavenly worshippers here on earth. May we say with John, "And I saw the holy city, New Jerusalem, coming down from God out of heaven, prepared as a bride adorned for her husband. And I heard a great voice out of heaven saying, Behold the tabernacle of God is with men, and He will dwell with them, and they shall be His people and God Himself shall be with them and be their God". [28]

Scripture References

1. Revelation 1: 17
2. Revelation 22: 3
3. Galatians 3: 13
4. Romans 8: 1
5. Genesis 3: 17-19
6. Psalm 77: 2

7. 1 Thess 5: 4-7
8. Isaiah 50: 10
9. Song of Sol 2: 17
9A. Rev. 22:5
9B. Rev. 21:1
10. Genesis 1: 10
11. Job 26: 10
12. Job 38: 11
13. Revelation 7: 16-17
14. Matthew 24: 7
15. Psalm 107: 5
16. Luke 4: 2
17. 1 Cor. 4: 11
18. Philippians 4: 11-12
19. Isaiah 58: 7
20. James 2: 15-17
21. Matthew 25: 46
22. John 6: 35
23. Matthew 5: 6
24. Psalm 42: 1-2
25. Isaiah 58: 11
26. Psalm 107: 9
27. Psalm 17: 15
28. Revelation 2: 2-4
29. Hebrews 2: 14-16
30. Matthew 8: 17
31. Isaiah 33: 24
32. John 11: 3
33. Philippians 4: 6-7
34. John 14: 27
35. Colossians 1: 20
36. John 11: 35-36
37. Psalm 56: 8
38. Psalm 30: 5
39. Joel 2: 1 and 12-18
40. Acts 20: 19
41. 2 Cor. 2: 4
42. Philippians 3: 18
43. John 20: 16
44. Romans 5: 12
45. Hebrews 9: 27
46. Romans 8: 1
47. Romans 6: 23
48. 2 Timothy 1: 10
49. 1 Cor. 15: 26
50. Revelation 14: 13
51. Revelation 20: 6
52. Proverbs 15: 24
53. Revelation 21: 22
54. Acts 20: 28
55. Revelation 7: 9
56. John 4: 21-24
57. Ezekiel 11: 16
58. Revelation 4: 10
59. Revelation 5: 9 and 12
60. Psalm 84: 1-4
61. Psalm 26: 8
62. Psalm 27: 4

9

What Heaven will Be

HEAVEN WILL BE A PLACE OF ROYAL RECEPTION

Christ has not forgotten His conversation with His disciples in the Upper Room concerning heaven. He said, "In my Father's house are many mansions: if it were not so, I would have told you. I go to prepare a place for you. And if I go and prepare a place for you, I will come again and receive you unto Myself, that where I am, there ye may be also."¹

Christ is going to come for us personally, and then receive us unto Himself. How rare, how unheard of for any King to come and take you to His palace. Christ is going to take us to His home and then it shall become ours. I have often thought upon "The unsearchable riches of Christ".² When we were young, we lived by the sea-side. Those caves became places of treasure and pebbles became stones of infinite value. By faith and the Spirit's leading how wonderful to search Christ's riches - to be daily led into "the depths of God". ³ - To find new caverns of Christ "In whom are hid all the treasures of wisdom and knowledge". ⁴ So in heaven, the Lord will take us down the corridors of His palace, from apartment to apartment, opening all the doors for us to gaze upon His glory. Then shall we know the total fulfilment of our prayer to Him, "Draw me, we will run after thee; the king hath brought me into his chambers". ⁵ That is a remarkable description of a royal reception. Then we shall actually sit at the table of the King of Kings, "While the king sitteth at his table, my spikenard sendeth forth the smell thereof". ⁵ In one sense it will be Christ supping with us, in another it will be our intimacy with Him, which will draw out devotion to God. A foretaste of heaven was known in the home in Bethany, where Christ shared the table with Mary, Martha and Lazarus, the Lazarus who had been raised from the dead. There they made the Lord a supper and Martha served, but Lazarus was one of them "that sat at the table **with Him**". [6] Like Mary, we offer our "ointment of spikenard very costly" and remember she "anointed the feet of Jesus, and wiped His feet with her hair: and the house was filled with the odour of the ointment." [6] Heaven will be full of the aroma of our devotion. The sweetest of which will be when He receives us in heaven. Heaven should be the greatest encouragement to us in this world. It should comfort our hearts, particularly concerning those who have died as true believers in Christ. "For the Lord Himself shall descend from heaven with a shout, with the voice of the archangel, and with the trump of God." [7] God uses Christ's return here, especially to comfort those who have lost loved ones who were in Christ.

The passage is so precious, so let Paul paint the picture in full. "But I would not have you ignorant brethren concerning them which are asleep that ye sorrow not, even as others which have no hope. For we believe that Christ died and rose again, even so them also that sleep in Jesus will God bring with him. For this we say unto you by the word of the Lord, that we which are alive and remain unto the coming of the Lord, shall not prevent them which are asleep". [7]

The final lead up to heaven is clear, that when the Lord descends with a shout (what a shout shall come from the Saviour's lips) and the trump of God, then there will be a resurrection of believers, "And the dead in Christ shall rise first". [7] God actually knows where the graves of Christians and non Christians are. As He said to Lazarus, "come forth and he that was dead came forth". [8] So likewise on that last day of earth Christ will speak to the very graves. Is it too marvellous in your eyes? Then it should not be, for Christ said nearly two thousand years ago, "Marvel not at this: for the hour is coming in the which all that are in the graves shall hear His voice, and shall come forth: they that have done good, unto the resurrection of life: and they that have done evil unto the resurrection of damnation". [9]

HEAVEN WILL BE A PLACE OF IMMEDIATE RECOGNITION

First we shall recognise Christ, the Lamb of God, though it will be the first time we have seen Him. Yet we are again assured, "Beloved, now are we the sons of God, and it doth not yet appear what we shall be: **but we know that when He shall appear, we shall be like Him**, for we shall see Him as He is". [10]

The hope of seeing Christ again and His heaven, is possibly the greatest incentive to Christ-likeness. May we realise that heaven is a place of purity. For the apostle of love wrote, "And every man that hath this hope in him, purifieth himself even as he is pure". [10], for nothing that defileth shall enter. But the question you are waiting to ask is, will we recognise our loved ones? To which Spurgeon is reported to have said, "Yes, because I won't be half the fool I am now!" Assuredly we shall, for as the old Sankey hymn says,

"We shall come with joy and gladness,
We shall gather round the throne,
Face to face with those who love us,
We shall know as we are known."

To me the great assurance is the Saviour's words firstly concerning those who have died thousands of years ago, "Now that the dead are raised, even Moses showed at the bush, when he called the Lord, the God of Abraham, and the God of Isaac and the God of Jacob. For He is not a God of the dead, but of the living; for all live unto Him". [11] Yes, you say, it's wonderful to know they are living and living unto Christ, but what about our knowing them and their knowing us? Well, Christ assures us that we "shall sit down with Abraham and Isaac and Jacob in the kingdom of heaven". [12] What a day that will be - actually to recognise and talk to Abraham. He will tell us what it was like to offer up his only son Isaac whom he loved. How at the final moment, God led him to draw back the knife. Again we shall ask, do you remember Christ coming with the angels and actually visiting you by your tent door in the plains of Mamre? There was a great old preacher called Rowland Hill, who was so eager to get to heaven, to speak to special people about special things. So one day when he was visiting a Christian who was very ill, he asked him to carry this message up to heaven. He said, "I hope they have not forgotten old Rowley (as he was affectionately known) and then he added, "Take my love up to the three glorious Johns, the Apostle John, John Bunyan and John Newton! Heaven will not only be a place of recognition, but a place of remembrance. We shall be like Christ and wonderfully remember things, as He did after His resurrection. He could say, "These are the words which I spoke unto you, while I was yet with you". [13] Surely the great hymn writer, Isaac Watts, was right when he wrote:-

"With transporting joys recount the labours of our feet"

3) HEAVEN WILL BE A PLACE OF REWARDS

The great returning victorious Roman generals like Pompey would have an abundant entrance back into their cities, with all their captives and spoil streaming behind them, as a defeated and pitiful sight. And in the Old Testament account of Christ's re-entry into the city of God above, we read, "The chariots of God are twenty thousand, even thousands of angels. The Lord is among them, as in Sinai, in the holy place. Thou hast ascended on high, thou hast led captivity captive". [14]

Likewise some Christians will have a rich entrance into heaven. Clearly all Christians will reach heaven, but not all will be rewarded with such an arrival. A Christian is to "Add to your faith virtue ... and knowledge ... and temperance, patience, godliness, brotherly kindness, charity". [15]

In the light of this new "furniture" for the apartment of our inner soul, it adds this terse exhortation, "Wherefore the rather brethren, give diligence to make your calling and election sure, for if ye do these things, ye shall never fall. For so an entrance shall be ministered unto you abundantly into the everlasting kingdom of our Lord and Saviour, Jesus Christ". [15]

Those who have lived in the light of the wisdom of God, and not followed the foolishness of their own fallen natures, shall shine as the stars, as the heavenly luminaries, as will also those who have spent their lives seeking to win souls for Christ, Who ultimately is the only true soul winner.

Fearfully Daniel describes the destiny of men set for heaven or hell. "And many of them that sleep in the dust of the earth shall awake, some to everlasting life, and some to shame and everlasting contempt". [16] Then follows a word about heavenly rewards, "And they that be wise shall shine as the brightness of the firmament, and they that turn many to righteousness as the stars for ever and ever". [16]

The persecuted godly will also receive rewards. Paul speaks of approaching "perilous times" and assures Christians that "all that will live godly shall suffer persecution". [17] No wonder Christ spoke of the ridiculed and reviled as rewarded Christians. The early Christians counted themselves "worthy to suffer for Christ's Name". [18] How comforting that He promised the pain of persecution would be recompensed by the happiness of heaven.

The Bible tells us that "Blessed are they which are persecuted for righteousness sake, for theirs is the Kingdom of Heaven. Blessed are ye when men shall revile you and persecute you and shall say all manner of evil against you falsely for my sake. Rejoice and be exceeding glad for great is your reward in heaven, for so persecuted they the prophets that were before you". [19]

Heaven for us will be largely determined by what we believed whilst on earth and also by what we did for God.

The Apostle Paul said of his Christian service that he had laid a foundation, which was Jesus Christ and there was no other. But he warned, "Let every man take heed how he buildeth thereon". [20]

He also said that our work for God here below would finally be proved by fire. If any man's work abide, which he hath built thereon, he shall receive a reward". But the opposite is fearfully true, "If any man's work shall be burnt, he shall suffer loss, yet he himself shall be saved; yet so as by fire". [20]

HEAVEN WILL BE A PLACE OF LIGHT

To the long list of "noes" in our negative approach to heaven in the previous chapter, we could have said no more sun and moon, for the light thereof is the Lamb of God, and heaven will be a place of everlasting spiritual illumination. "And the city had no need of the sun nor of the moon to shine in it, for the glory of God did lighten it". [21]

The shining Saviour will draw and make heaven to be the place of saved souls out of all the nations of the world. They will be basking eternally in the light of God's Lamb, and even saved Kings and leaders of the nations shall be acknowledged there.

HEAVEN WILL BE A PLACE OF REJOICING

When we reach heaven, God will say "Enter thou into the joy of thy Lord". [22] It is to be in the presence of God with His servants. "In Thy presence is fulness of joy; at Thy right hand there are pleasures for evermore". [23]

HEAVEN WILL BE A PLACE OF ANGELIC WORSHIP

Heaven is not merely a state of mind as some modern men will have it, but it is a place - not merely worth visiting - but finally to live in for ever. Just imagine arriving there. We shall find it not only full of people, but angels too. We are given in the Bible a picture of the company we shall enjoy. It is like the Jerusalem below, "Beautiful for situation, the joy of the whole earth is mount Zion". [24] A striking feature will be the mountainous terrain, "Ye are come unto mount Sion", [25] but it is also the city above all cities, the capital of heaven, for we have come to "the city of the living God". [25] All the other cities we have known have been marked by decadence, destruction and death. But the life of the living God will pulsate through the whole population of that city, for its heartbeat will be the pure and exciting one of God Himself, duly to be enjoyed. You are entering nothing less than the heavenly Jerusalem, then suddenly you meet with "an innumerable company of angels". [25] Elsewhere in the last book of the Bible, we catch a glimpse of the angels in action, literally millions singing loudly the worth of the Lord Jesus. Even Handel will be speechless with admiration when he hears the heavenly hallelujah chorus. John caught up in a God-given vision of the scene from his exile on Patmos, describes vividly the picture he was permitted to see. He says "I beheld and I heard the voice of many angels round about the throne and the beasts and the elders, and the number of them was ten thousand times ten thousand and thousands of thousands of thousands saying with a loud voice Worthy is the Lamb". [26]

HEAVEN WILL BE THE GATHERING PLACE FOR THE CHURCH OF ALL NATIONS

Then we shall say, "There they are". The Church of all ages, patriarchs, prophets, apostles, martyrs, and Christians of all colours, kindred and tribes will be there, an international company. We have caught the Church in heavenly session, for we are come "to the general assembly and church of the first born, which are written in heaven". [25] We shall see our first Sunday School teacher, those who were our beloved pastors, the missionaries who went at God's bidding to the ends of the earth. Isn't that Livingstone? Surely that is Brainerd, and that must be John Paton. There are Abraham, Isaac and Jacob, still linked together as on earth. Only one man could have a voice like that. Yes, it's Charles Haddon Spurgeon. But who is that? It is none other than yourself, if you are one of those who in this life "have washed their robes and made them white in the blood of the Lamb". [27] You may never be in the "Who's Who" in this world, but it is essential that you are numbered among those who are "written in heaven". Once in Christ's lifetime there was an amazing moment when seventy men surrounded Him, all of them trying to attract His attention and pour out their excited words of success. Who are they, do you ask? They are preachers of God, His seventy sign-posts, who have been on a mission for their Master, to try and win that part of the world for Him. Just listen to them - "And the seventy returned again with joy, saying, Lord even the devils are subject to us through Thy name". [28] But suddenly Christ hushes them with one of the most remarkable utterances that ever fell from His lips during His thirty-three years on earth. "Notwithstanding, in this rejoice not, that the spirits are subject unto you; but rather rejoice that your names are written in heaven". [28]

Go back hundreds of years before this. Here is Moses breaking his heart over man without God and without hope of salvation, for he knows that unless they are saved, they will not be in God's book of life. He then shows a passion for the souls rare in any man in any century. He is willing to sacrifice his heaven for lost souls. He is willing to have his name removed from the book of life, that someone else in his place may enjoy heaven. These are amazing words as he speaks to God. "Yet now, if thou wilt forgive their sin - ; and, if not, blot me, I pray thee out of thy book which thou hast written". [29]

HEAVEN WILL BE A PLACE OF PERFECT LOVE

Heaven, in a word, is a world of love. Christ in that great prayer before His death, uttered this petition, "That they may behold my glory, which thou hast given me, for thou lovest me before the foundation of the world". [30] He then summarised what He did for men whilst He was on earth, and what He desires for man in heaven - "I have declared unto them thy name, and will declare it, **that the love wherewith thou hast loved me** may be in them and I in them". [30] Truly it has been written "God is love"", [31] and "the greatest of these is love". [32] Yes, as we have seen heaven can begin here, and never was this more true.

Not long before Christ died, He gathered His beloved disciples together in a spacious upper room in Jerusalem and told them how heaven could begin here and its love to be born in them. His actual words were these, "As my Father hath loved Me, so have I loved you: continue ye in My love. If ye keep My commandments, ye shall abide in My love, even as I have kept My Father's commandments and abide in His love". [33] Christ literally lived in heavenly love with His Father, whilst He walked through this old world. So can we if we only obey Him.

The love of God from Heaven is revealed in three different ways. There is a common grace or love to all people. Common, not in some inferior sense, but in that it is common to all people, whether they acknowledge it or not. For "God maketh his sun to rise on the evil and on the good and sendeth rain on the just and on the unjust". [34] Again, "The Lord is good to all and His tender mercy is over all His works". [35] Then beyond that there is His redeeming love. It is amazing that God revealed His love, His dying love to His enemies, to a world that at the best had no time for Him and certainly never invited Him into it, let alone to die for their sins. "But, God commendeth His love towards us, in that while we were **yet sinners** Christ died for us". [36] And again the apostle of love wrote long ago, "Herein is love, not that we loved God, but that He loved us and sent His son to be the propitiation for our sins", [37] which leads a saved sinner in this twentieth century to come to this logical conclusion, "We love Him because He first loved us". [37]

But let us now come to the fatherly and heavenly love that Christ in measure granted us on earth, as a foretaste of that love, both ahead of us and above us. Christ says, "As the Father hath loved Me". [33] You have to look into heaven to discover how the Father loves the Son. It is a father-son love, a filial family love. This certainly was not redeeming love, for it would be blasphemous, for the Father never loved the Son as a sinner. For Christ is "holy, harmless, undefiled and separate from sinners". [38] God said it all to His Son in those never to be forgotten words, "Thou art My beloved Son, in whom I am well pleased", [39] - literally as the one **having been** loved. There was never a time when God did not love His Son. And now as Christians, He treats us as He treats His Son, and loves us as He loved Him. Are there two greater comforts than these? Finally we can know that we are united with the Son of God's love and therefore, He never sees us, nor deals with us outside of Christ. We are "accepted in the beloved". [40] God never sees us alone, but always in His Son, and He never loves Him without shedding His love also upon us. The liquid love of heaven can be poured into our hearts today. Are we asking, how will God love us in heaven? The answer - as He loves His Son now. This heavenly love is, therefore, freely to be found in America, Asia, or in Africa, as in England, as much as in heaven.

It is necessary to say, to be fair, there is a difference between the Father's love for His only begotten Son, and that for us. Of the Son He says, "Thou art my Son, this day I have begotten thee", [41] whereas we are creatures of God's creation. Likewise, Christ is a natural son, whilst we are adopted into the Royal family of heaven. Having said all that, we must never loose sight of the likeness. God loves us as His Son. Therefore, it is an eternal love, without a beginning and without an ending. Incredibly He assures us "I have loved thee with an everlasting love". [42] Now if that is just too much for us to take in, or even more, if you say, at least prove it to me that God has loved me with the same heavenly love, as He does His Son, then read on. "Therefore, with loving kindness have I drawn thee". [42] The love of God which draws us to Christ in time, is proof of His timeless love for us. We are meant to trace the thread of love from our hearts on earth to His heart in heaven. These words so captivated Nicola's mother after her little daughter had died of leukaemia, that she scribbled down these words "Nicola - living in everlasting love". If you climb the hill outside Guildford - it is rather like the Hill Difficulty with House Beautiful on top - you will not only travel the Pilgrim Way again, but you will find a tiny tomb-stone with those words upon it.

We can capture something of the way God loved His Son in heaven before He became a man on earth. Christ had recorded something of that time, "Then I was by Him as one brought up with Him: and I was daily His delight, rejoicing always before Him". [43] Here we have the picture of Christ revelling in His Father's love. Oh! how we need that today. You may say, what can heaven find to love in me? Well, that is certainly true of us, but it has been rightly said that the first reason for God's love for man is outside of man and therefore eternal. God chose us, because He loves us. "The Lord did not set His love upon you, nor choose you, because you were more in number than any people ... but because He loved you". [44] God loves you because of Christ, for He said His Father had loved us, as He loved Christ, "before the foundation of the world". [45]

Heaven's love is an unchanging love. Here on earth we say, "Lord it is my chief complaint, that my love is weak and faint ... O for grace to love

Thee more". But the heavenly love is as unchanging as God Himself. God loves His Son with an equal love, not more one day than another, and it is that love we can experience here upon earth and in the world to come. Through sin here, we can lose the consciousness of it, but nothing will mar God's felt love there. His "Perfect love casteth out fear". [46] His love is always the same, and is the only answer to fear in the heart of man. "Jesus Christ the same yesterday, and today, and for ever". [47] Oh! let God say to you today, "I am the Lord, I change not; therefore ye sons of Jacob are not consumed". [48]

Another glorious quality of the heavenly love, is that it is without limits. We have earlier thought of the love the early Christians knew in the midst of the hatred of their evil persecutors. Those in the Neronian persecution knew both heavenly love and joy upholding them - "Whom having not seen ye love, yet believing ye rejoice, with joy unspeakable and full of glory". [49]

The great apostle put down his pen in the midst of a letter he was writing to a church and prayed, "That Christ may dwell in your hearts by faith, that ye being rooted and grounded in love may be able to comprehend with all saints what is the breadth and length and depth and height and to know the love of Christ, which passeth knowledge". [50] Heaven's love surpasses the greatest knowledge of God we can know in this world. The great evangelist, Dwight Moody, who had broad and massive shoulders, had such an experience of God one day in his life, that he had to ask God to hold back His love, because he felt it would break him and he could not take any more.

In an earlier century, Thomas Goodwin, the Puritan, sought to describe this heavenly love. He painted the picture of a father walking along a road with his son. They were holding hands, because they loved each other. Then he described how suddenly the father felt such a sense of love for his son in his heart, that merely holding hands was no longer sufficient to express his feeling for the lad. So, there and then, he swept the boy off his feet and held him to his breast. Now their relationship had not changed, but the expression of it had vastly altered. These are but foretastes here on this earth of heaven's world of love.

Be assured that sometimes God comes to us as He came to Daniel of old on more than one occasion, and said, "O man greatly beloved, fear not: peace be unto thee, be strong, yea be strong. And when He had spoken unto me, I was strengthened, and said 'Let my Lord speak, for Thou hast strengthened me.'"[51] When this happens no man can ever be quite the same again in this world and longs to be found again in that world of love.

Heaven's love will be unending. It says of Christ reclining with His disciples in His last private disclosure with them, "When Jesus knew that His hour was come that he should depart out of this world unto the Father, having loved His own, which were in the world, He loved them unto the end". [52] Even in ancient times God's people knew that "The mercy of the Lord is from everlasting to everlasting upon them that fear Him". [53]

If we are to know earthly foretastes of heaven's love, we must fulfil Christ's sole condition - that of obedience. "If ye keep My commandments, ye shall abide in My love, even as I have kept My Father's commandments and abide in His love". [54] The late Dr. A.W. Tozer put it in an incredibly challenging way, "The Christian cannot be certain of the reality of His love until he come face to face with the commandments of Christ and is forced to decide what to do about them."

The proof of our love is not feeling, but doing. Christ during the whole of His life on earth, lived in obedience to His Father's commandments, and, therefore, always lived and moved in the sphere of heavenly love, and His word is still relevant to us today, that the condition of abiding in His love is obedience.

Christ's life secret may be summarised in these words, "The Father hath not left Me alone, for I do always those thing that please Him". [55] Even His death and resurrection were acts of loving obedience to God His Father. He declared "Therefore doth My Father love Me, because I lay down My life that I might take it again. No man taketh it from Me. I have power to lay down My life that I might take it again. No man taketh it from Me. I have power to lay it down and I have power to take it again. This commandment have I received of My Father". [56]

In His daily obedience to His Father, He never forgot why He had come down from heaven. His human will was ever in subjection to God, in that He could say, "I came down from heaven, not to do My own will, but the will of Him that sent me". [57] Even His very speech, His every word was spoken in the will of God. Self never seasoned His conversation for He declared, "For I have spoken not of Myself, but My Father which sent Me, He gave me commandment what I should say and what I should speak". [58] So, shortly before His crucifixion, He uttered these remarkable words in prayer, "I have glorified Thee on the earth, I have finished the work which

Thou gavest Me to do".⁵⁹ Yes, He did abide in His Father's love, by keeping His commandments. He glorified His Father by finishing His work. Such a life of obedience will lead us to the experience of knowing God's heavenly love on earth. Let us never forget His words, "He that hath My commandments and keepeth them, he it is that loveth Me ... and I will love him and manifest Myself to him".⁶⁰

One recalls the words of one of the greatest missionaries of all time - John Paton - who went to the South Sea islands, the New Hebrides. There he was surrounded by cannibals who literally at times tried to strike off his head with their hatchets. When he was miraculously delivered, he came to realise in a moment of quiet contemplation, in his own words, "I was immortal until my work was done".

> "In heavenly love abiding,
> No change my heart shall fear,
> And safe is such confiding,
> For nothing changes here.
> The storm may roar without me,
> My heart may low be laid,
> But God is round about me,
> And can I be dismayed."

HEAVEN WILL BE A PLACE OF GLORY

Although heaven is a place where the glory of God is, yet it is a glory of which we shall be a part. This will be, not only to be with Christ for ever, but like Him for ever. The sheer anticipation of that should drive us to become more Christ-like, in all we do and say and think, but above all in what we really are. We should often pray the verse of the hymn:-

> "O Jesus Christ grow Thou in me,
> And all things else recede."

Again our aim should be, as that of John of old, "He must increase, but I must decrease".⁶¹ That is not just a passing resolution or aspiration of a man of God, but rather the purpose of the God of man for our life, which He has defined in that "He did predestinate (choose with the end in view) to be conformed to the image of his son".⁶²

How differently we would live here below if we realised that all man's distresses, problems, troubles and the hard things we have to undertake is God's seeking to form the life and character of Christ in us. Paul could say of the Christians of his day, "My little children, of whom I travail in birth until **Christ be formed in you**". [63] Perhaps this day you feel like giving up. Oh! believe in Christ your Saviour and look up through the darkness that shrouds you and trust His word, "We shall be like Him, for we shall see Him as He is". [64] Recall at this moment Christ's promise, "that where I am, there ye may be also". [65] Not long before He was crucified, He prayed the most heavenly prayer that ever fell from the lips of man. He wanted us not only to be with Him in glory, but to see what He sees. John was permitted to eavesdrop upon the prayer for you and me. It began like this, "Father I will that they also whom Thou hast given Me **be with Me where I am**, that they may behold My glory which Thou hast given Me …"[66]

How wonderful to wake up in the morning with that incredible and comforting thought in mind, forming itself in to this prayer, "May my life this day be but the fulfilment of Christ's promise and the answer to His prayer". It has already been mentioned that we should be with Him where He is, and also this prayer of His, "that they may behold My glory". Those are the only two things you can be sure of today and indeed from now to the endless day of heaven - His promises and His prayers, which can bring heaven to you here and ultimately take you to heaven there. I know of only one greater comfort and that is to look up and know there is a Man in heaven praying for me to reach where He is. In the "impossible" hopeless days, that is my only stay.

"**But this Man**, because He continueth ever, hath an unchangeable priesthood, Wherefore He is able also to save them to the uttermost that come unto God by Him, seeing He ever liveth to make intercession for them".[67]

Since being back in heaven, Christ has continuously prayed for His people, that they might come and be with Him and like Him. I find that unbelievably beautiful and beneficial in this vale of tears and often slough of despond.

I shall never forget a man in my first church who didn't come to faith in Christ as his Saviour until he was about fifty. He had a long, painful illness, but it drove him to the "Rock of Ages" for shelter and he sucked honey out of that Rock. The day before he died, he looked out across the still waters of the little lake at the bottom of his garden, and simply said with the simplicity of a child, "Paul, I shall see the Lord Jesus and be with Him". Now that it is the way we should live and die. Then you will have this assurance, "I shall be satisfied, when I awake, with Thy likeness". Earth is a place of great dissatisfaction, because we are so unlike Christ. To be like Him, is to be able to say He satisfies.

Scripture References

1. John 14: 2, 3
2. Ephesians 3: 8
3. 1 Corinthians 2: 10
4. Colossians 2: 3
5. Song of Sol. 1: 4
Song of Sol. 1: 12
6. John 12: 2
John 12: 3
7. 1 Thess. 4: 13-16
8. John 11: 43, 44
9. John 5: 28, 29
10. 1 John 3: 2, 3
11. Luke 20: 37, 38
12. Matthew 8: 11
13. Luke 24: 44
14. Psalm 68: 17, 18
15. 2 Peter 1: 5-7
2 Peter 1: 10, 11
16. Daniel 12: 2, 3
17. 2 Timothy 3: 12
18. Acts 5: 41
19. Matthew 5: 10-12
20. 1 Corinthians 3: 10, 11
1 Corinthians 3: 14, 15
21. Revelation 21: 23
22. Matthew 25: 21
23. Psalm 16: 11
24. Psalm 48: 2
25. Hebrews 12: 22-24
26. Revelation 5: 11, 12
27. Revelation 7: 14
28. Luke 10: 17 and 20
29. Exodus 32: 32
30. John 17: 24 and 26
31. 1 John 4: 5
32. 1 Corinthians 13: 13
33. John 15: 9, 10
34. Matthew 5: 45
35. Psalm 145: 9
36. Romans 5: 8
37. 1 John 4: 10
1 John 4: 19
38. Hebrews 7: 26
39. Luke 3: 22
40. Ephesians 1: 6
41. Psalm 2: 7
42. Jeremiah 31: 3
43. Proverbs 8: 30
44. Deuteronomy 7: 7
45. Ephesians 1: 4
46. 1 John 4: 18
47. Hebrews 13: 8
48. Malachi 3: 6
49. 1 Peter 1: 8
50. Ephesians 3: 17-19
51. Daniel 10: 19
52. John 13: 1
53. Psalm 103: 17
54. John 15: 10
55. John 8: 29
56. John 10: 17, 18
57. John 6: 38
58. John 12: 49
59. John 17: 4
60. John 14: 21
61. John 3: 30
62. Romans 8: 29
63. Galatians 4: 19
64. 1 John 3: 2
65. John 14: 3
66. John 17: 24
67. Hebrews 7: 24

10

Heaven - A New World

"And I saw a new heaven and a new earth, for the first heaven and the first earth were passed away". [1] Heaven is a new world, but in a sense not totally new. It will be a world purged of every corrupting influence of sin, sickness, sorrow and death. It will be rejuvenated, renewed and refreshed by God. As for our bodies, "We shall be changed". [2] So too will this world for, "The whole creation groaneth and travaileth in pain together until now"; [3] it longs to be rid of the curse of sin and have it purged away for ever. We must recall that when man first sinned, the whole creation fell with man. God said to Adam, "Because thou hast hearkened unto the voice of thy wife and hast eaten of the tree of which I commanded you not to eat, cursed is the ground for thy sake: in sorrow shalt thou eat of it all the days of thy life, thorns and thistles shall it bring forth to thee, and thou shalt eat of the herb of the field". [4] So from the day man sinned, his daily work became a burden and hard labour to him. For God told him, "In the sweat of thy face shalt thou eat bread, till thou return unto the ground; for out of it wast thou taken; for dust thou art and unto dust shalt thou return". [5]

THE NEW HEAVENS AND THE NEW EARTH

In the new heavens and the new earth, we shall see the state of the world restored, to be more glorious than the original Garden of Eden. For the world will never decay again, for in heaven man will never sin again. It will be beautiful, planted and cultivated by God Himself, so will be full of wonderful trees and gardens, watered by rivers sweetly flowing through them. God's description indeed is heavenly - "For behold I create new heavens and a new earth, and the former shall not be remembered, nor come to mind. But be ye glad and rejoice for ever in that which I create, for behold I create Jerusalem a rejoicing, and her people a joy".[6]

This new world which will bring the heavenly city of Jerusalem to be entitled "A rejoicing" and its people "a joy" will cause the misery of sin to be immediately replaced by the joy of God. The city in heaven will never know sorrow and unhappiness. No policeman will walk its streets, no sirens of ambulances will be heard. It will be utterly safe to walk out without fear of violence. In fact it is said, "No lion shall be there, nor any ravenous beast shall go up thereon, it shall not be found there, but the redeemed of the Lord shall walk there. And the ransomed of the Lord shall return and come to Zion with songs and everlasting joy upon their heads; they shall obtain joy and gladness and sorrow and sighing shall flee away".[7]

ANIMALS IN HEAVEN

Immediately you notice that the animal kingdom is no longer fallen and fierce. It will have been "tamed" and restored to its original perfection. At the beginning of the creation of the world, Adam had the unenviable task of giving the animals names for God. The lion, the tiger and the bear, with more timid animals were brought to Adam to name them. It says that "Out of the ground the Lord God formed every beast of the field, and every fowl of the air, and brought them unto Adam to see what he would call them; and whatsoever Adam called every living creature, that was the name thereof".[8] Such a thing would be madness and highly dangerous to do now. But Adam handled them before the fall and the fierceness had not entered them. You will hardly believe your eyes when you see animals in heaven, not in any zoo, but running wild and "The wolf and the lamb shall feed together".[6] Only in a new world could that happen. It is amazing enough to see them together, but feeding is even more unbelievable, because the wolf would normally feed upon the lamb! And over there, is another incredible sight, for "The lion shall eat straw like the bullock, and dust shall be the serpent's meat".[6] Then the real clue to all this change to animal life-style is given in a word, "They shall not hurt nor destroy in all My holy mountain",[6] and we have already seen that no lion or ravenous beast will be there. God says concerning the people, "I will rejoice in Jerusalem and joy in my people; and the voice of weeping shall be no more heard in her, nor the voice of crying". [6]

The whole problem of ageing and growing old with dignity so called, will no longer be a live issue "For there shall be no more thence an infant of days, nor an old man". [6]

Heavenly man shall not be inactive we are told, "And they shall build houses and inhabit them, and they shall plant vineyards and eat the fruit of them. They shall not build and another inhabit; they shall not plant and another eat: For as the days of a tree are the days of my people, and Mine elect shall long enjoy the work of their hands". [6] It is difficult to be too definite regarding this great chapter, but it clearly goes beyond the idea of merely a glorious golden age for the Church on earth before the coming of the Lord. And again, God says, "For as the new heavens and the new earth which I will make shall remain before Me, saith the Lord, so shall your seed and your name remain". [9]

GREAT CONFLAGRATION

Peter at the end of the New Testament draws out the spiritual lessons for us. He speaks of such a great momentous event when, in some great conflagration the world will be purged as by fire. "But the heavens and the earth which are now, by the same word are kept in store, reserved unto fire against the day of judgment and perdition of ungodly men. But beloved be not ignorant of this one thing, that one day is with the Lord as a thousand years, and a thousand years as one day. The Lord is not slack concerning his promise, as some men count slackness; but is long-suffering to us-ward, not willing that any should perish, but that all should come to repentance". [10]

Peter tells us that the return of the Lord will come as a thief in the night, without obvious warning, "In the which the heavens will pass away with a great noise and the elements shall melt with fervent heat, the earth also and the works that are therein shall be burned up".[10] Surely God does not want us to waste our time considering whether it is a hydrogen or a neutron bomb and what will be the effects of it. In fact, God's purpose by the fire is not destructive, but purgative. As Peter says, "Nevertheless, we, according to His promise, look for new heavens and a new earth, wherein dwelleth righteousness". [10] This is meant for us to seek to be as righteous as the new heavens and the new earth. For he continues, "Wherefore, beloved, seeing that ye look for such things, be diligent that ye may be found of Him in peace without spot and blameless. And account that the longsuffering of the Lord is salvation ..." [10] Earlier he takes a similar line of warning, advocating preparation to face God, Who is purging the earth and the heavens, "Seeing that all these things shall be dissolved, what manner of persons ought ye to be in all holy conversation and godliness". [10]

A NEW HOME IN HEAVEN

How often the Church is caught up like its politicians and militarists, in debating the bomb, rather than preparing the people to be ready to move into a new home in heaven. Anything beyond this, is man's surmising and idle speculation. Thank God, in heaven there will be an end of war of all kinds, small or great. "And it shall come to pass in the last days that the mountain of the Lord's house shall be established in the top of the mountains, and shall be exalted above the hills, and all nations shall flow unto it! And many people shall go and say, Come ye, let us go up to the mountain of the Lord, to the house of the God of Jacob; and He will teach us of His ways, and we will walk in His paths, for out of Zion shall go forth the law, and the word of the Lord from Jerusalem. And He shall judge among the nations, and shall rebuke many people, and they shall beat their swords into plowshares and their spears into pruning hooks. Nation shall not lift up sword against nation, neither shall they learn war any more". [11]

Until man is finally and totally redeemed, and the last dregs of sin removed from him, we shall have wars and rumours of wars, and no international planning will change the heart of man. For God makes it so plain when He says, "From whence come wars and fightings amongst you? Come they not hence, even of your lusts that war in your members. Ye lust and ye have not, and kill and desire to have, and cannot obtain, ye fight and war, yet ye have not, because ye ask not". [12]

PERFECT GOVERNMENT

Oh! roll on "new heaven and new earth, in which dwelleth righteousness!" Then there will be a new and perfect government. A godly man, Richard Hooker, near the end of his life said, "I go to a world of order". Only then will our Christ-given prayer be fully answered, "Thy will be done, in earth, as it is in heaven". [13] When Christ left the door of heaven open, John was given the privilege of looking in, and the first thing he saw and recorded was, "Behold a door was open in heaven ... and behold a throne was set in heaven". [14] The rule of God in all His purity and power, is meant to create voiced praise in our lives and upon our lips. We are meant to be joining already with those around the Throne of God, and crying "Alleluia, for the Lord God omnipotent reigneth". [15]

HEAVENLY SERVICE

We may have had no part in local, national or European government on earth, but every Christian will in heaven, for it is not only a place of service, but such service is specifically defined. We are told "His servants shall serve Him", [16] which incidentally does away with the idea of sitting at ease in heaven. Firstly we shall have a part in the judgment of the world. We are rudely awakened from dreams of an eternity of ease, by the personal and pertinent question, "Do you not know that the saints shall judge the world?"[17] And before we recover from reeling under that question, another comes quickly upon its heels, "Know ye not that ye shall judge angels?"[17] In heaven we shall be serving as rulers. There is decidedly a recognition of services rendered on earth, which will prepare us for greater responsibilities above. In that connection, Christ says, "His lord said unto him, well done, good and faithful servant: thou hast been faithful over a few things, I will make thee a ruler over many things, enter thou into the joy of thy lord".[18]

A NEW MARRIAGE

In heaven there will be a new marriage. For a true and vital understanding of this, we must once more hear the words of Christ Himself, "But they which shall be accounted worthy to obtain that world and the resurrection from the dead, neither marry, nor are given in marriage, neither can they die any more: for they are equal unto the angels; and are the children of God, being the children of the resurrection". [19]

Have you never seen that the relationship of Christ to the Church is that of a bridegroom to a bride, "that ye should be married to another, even to Him who is raised from the dead, that we should bring forth fruit unto

God".[20] Way back in ancient times, God assured the Church, "Your Maker is your husband".[21]

In the last book of the Bible, heaven is set forth as God's marriage day. We are invited as God's bride, the Church, to "be glad and rejoice and give honour to Him, for the marriage of the Lamb is come, and His bride hath made herself ready".[15]

Readiness means that we are robed in the pure white wedding dress of God, which is His own righteous robe, given to us the day we believe in Him in this world, and yet to be worn throughout eternity. It will be a heavenly honeymoon, which shall know no end; the bride shall never take off her wedding dress, but wear it for ever to please her bridegroom, who made it for her and beautified her for all eternity. No wonder elsewhere it says, "The King's daughter is all glorious within and her clothing is wrought gold".[22] No wonder it says, "Shall the King greatly desire thy beauty, for He is thy Lord, worship thou Him".[22] Oh! to her (to you dear Christian) was granted that she should be arrayed in fine linen, clean and white for the fine linen is the righteousness of the saints".[15]

> "Jesus, Thy robe of righteousness
> My beauty are, my glorious dress;
> Midst flaming worlds in these arrayed,
> With joy shall I lift up my head
>
> Bold shall I stand in that great day
> For who aught to my charge shall lay?
> Fully absolved through, Thee I am
> From sin and fear, from guilt and shame.
>
> This spotless robe the same appears,
> When ruined nature sinks in years;
> No age can change its glorious hue,
> The robe of Christ is ever new.
>
> When from the dust of death I rise
> To claim my mansion in the skies,
> E'en then shall this be all my plea
> 'Jesus hath lived and died for me.'

> O let the dead now hear Thy voice!
> Now bid Thy banished ones rejoice!
> Their beauty this, their glorious dress,
> Jesus, the Lord our righteousness."

Robert Murray McCheyne, who has vowed by God's grace that he would be as holy as a pardoned sinner might be, was in heaven at the age of 29. He left behind him this beautiful legacy of love and he was ready "to stand with Christ on high" because he was, in his own words, "dressed in beauty not my own". He too had on Christ's wedding garment.

> "When this passing world is done,
> When has sunk yon radiant sun,
> When I stand with Christ on high,
> Looking o'er life's history,
> Then, Lord shall I fully know,
> Not till then, how much I owe.
>
> When I stand before the throne,
> Dressed in beauty not my own,
> When I see Thee as Thou art,
> Love Thee with unsinning heart,
> Then, Lord, shall I fully know,
> Not till then, how much I owe.
>
> When the praise of heaven I hear,
> Loud as thunders to the ear,
> Loud as many waters' noise,
> Sweet as harp's melodious voice,
> Then, Lord, shall I fully know,
> Not till then, how much I owe.
>
> Chosen, not for good in me.
> Wakened up from wrath to flee,
> Hidden in the Saviour's side,
> By the Spirit sanctified,
> Teach me, Lord, on earth, to show,
> by my love, how much I owe."

Many Christ-like men and women have anticipated the marriage supper of the Lamb in heaven. None more than Samuel Rutherford, who was imprisoned for the gospel in Scotland in the 17th century. There he wrote the most precious letters setting forth the loveliness of Christ and of heaven ahead. Anne Cousin extracted some of these gems and put them in her poem, "In Immanuel's Land".

"The Bride eyes not her garment,
But her dear Bridegroom's face;
I will not gaze at glory,
But on my King of grace;
Not at the crown He giveth,
But on His pierced hand:
The Lamb is all the glory,
Of Immanuel's land."

THE GREAT WHITE THRONE

There is a story told of a man named Eddie who from a godless life, having found the Lord Jesus Christ, fell completely in love with Him. Working on the railway as a signalman, he used, when he had opportunity, to call a friend in the next signal box along the line, to talk to him on his favourite theme of his wonderful Saviour, and how he hoped he would come to know Him too.

One day, he inadvertently touched a switch which opened up the whole area to his conversation about Christ. For miles around people heard about God and His great white throne, before which we must all appear one day. When it was traced to Eddie, everywhere people would ask him the meaning of what he had said.

Eventually he was called before the manager, known to be a strict disciplinarian, who turning to Eddie said, "What is this about a great white throne?" As Eddie unashamedly spoke of his glorious friend and Saviour, the senior railway official was deeply moved.

In the end, he opened his heart to Eddie and told him he was shortly to undergo a serious operation. Without a word, the two men knelt together and the manager poured out his heart to a merciful and pardoning God upon a great white throne.

THE MARRIAGE SUPPER OF THE LAMB

Eddie became quite famous in his area, always testifying to Christ wherever he went, and was amazed to receive an invitation for a luncheon in Chester Castle which the Queen would attend. Alas, poor Eddie! He had read that he was invited to the luncheon, but had failed to see that morning dress was required. Imagine his dismay when at the castle gates, he was barred from entry by two crossed pikes, and a guard gruffly saying, "You can't go in there; you are not properly dressed". Dejected Eddie turned away. Then suddenly an arm was put round him, and a Christian friend, a local police officer, said, "It's alright Eddie, you'll get to see the King of kings, because you have your wedding garment on". He was of course, referring to the wedding supper of Christ, and the necessity of having on the robe of Christ's perfect righteousness. Indeed, "Blessed are they who are called to the wedding supper of the Lamb". [15] Eddie would be one who would certainly qualify, and we must ask ourselves, would we?

PERFECT WORSHIP

The most wonderful thing about heaven, however, will be the perfect, endless, ceaseless worship of Christ, the Lamb of God. Time will be no more. What a hindrance it has often been to the true worship of God in this world! One of our dying regrets will surely be that we have worshipped too much in the light of time and to little in the light of eternity. John Bunyan, the immortal dreamer, wrote in "Pilgrim's Progress", "Now just as the gates were opened to let in the men, I looked in after them and behold the city shone like the sun, the streets also were paved with gold, and in them walked many men with crowns on their heads, palms in their hands, and golden harps to play withal. There was also of them that had wings and they answered one another without intermission saying, 'Holy, Holy, Holy is the Lord' ... which when I had seen, I wished myself amongst them".

It will truly be perfect worship, because we shall have a perfect vision of God for the first time. "But now we see through a glass darkly, but then face to face. Now I know in part, but then shall I know, even as I am known". [23]

Yet, daily we should say, "Perhaps today" my Lord will return to this world. We must even now, by faith, gaze upon glory and be changed into the glorious likeness of God in greater degree. "But we all with open face, beholding in a glass the glory of the Lord are changed into the same image from glory to glory, even as by the Spirit of the Lord". [24]

Oh! the greatest thing about glory will be when we "shall see HIS FACE". [16] Even though we have to confess "It doth not yet appear what we shall be". [25] How true and realistic are the words of Richard Baxter.

"My knowledge of that life is small,
The eye of faith is dim,
It is enough that Christ knows all,
And I shall be with Him."

Or with Charles Wesley's fine verse,

"Finish then Thy new creation,
Pure and spotless may we be:
Let us see Thy great salvation,
Perfectly restored in Thee,
Changed from glory into glory,
Till in heaven we take our place,
Till we cast our crowns before Thee,
Lost in wonder, live and praise."

GLORIOUS BODY

We shall worship in that great day in a new body, for Christ "shall change our vile body, that it might be fashioned like unto His glorious body, according to the working whereby He is able to subdue all things unto Himself". [26] And again we read of Christ's final action "Then cometh the end, when He shall have delivered up the kingdom to God, even the Father; when He shall have put down all rule and authority and power. For He must reign, till He hath put all enemies under His feet. The last enemy that shall be destroyed is death ... and when all things shall be subdued unto Him, then shall the Son also himself be subject unto Him, that God may be all in all". [27]

Christ's mediatorial work will be finished for ever. Heaven will be finished here on earth, but it will be only just beginning above. The only way we can finish this book on heaven, is praying for heaven to come and also for the Christ of heaven to come back and take us to be with Him for ever.

"He which testifieth these things saith, Surely I come quickly. Amen. Even so, come Lord Jesus". [28]

THE ULTIMATE

- YOU MUST BE FORCED TO COME TO THE END OF MAN BEFORE YOU FIND GOD.
- YOU MUST BE FORCED TO COME TO THE END OF EARTH BEFORE YOU FIND HEAVEN.
- YOU MUST BE FORCED TO COME TO THE END OF YOURSELF BEFORE YOU FIND HIMSELF.

Scripture References

1. Revelation 21: 1
2. 1 Corinth. 15: 52
3. Romans 8: 22
4. Genesis 3: 17, 18
5. Genesis 3: 19
6. Isaiah 65: 17, 18
7. Isaiah 35: 9, 10
8. Genesis 2: 19
9. Isaiah 66: 22
10. 2 Peter 3: 7-15
11. Isaiah 2: 2-4
12. James 4: 1, 2
13. Matthew 6: 10
14. Revelation 4: 1, 2
15. Revelation 19: 6-9
16. Revelation 22: 3, 4
17. 1 Corinth. 6: 2, 3
18. Matthew 25: 21
19. Luke 20: 35, 36
20. Romans 7: 4
21. Isaiah 54: 5
22. Psalm 45: 11 and 13
23. 1 Corinth. 13: 12
24. 2 Corinth. 3: 18
25. 1 John 3: 2
26. Philippians 3: 21
27. 1 Corinth. 15: 24-28
28. Revelation 22: 20